Ethics
Study guide

Peter Baron

Contents

Purpose of the Book

The OCR 2016 specification H573 has posed some challenges for teacher and student, and for this reason this guide represents the foundation of a new approach to study which integrates elements of the Peped project to make creative learning of philosophy accessible to everyone.

- The textbooks have produced their own interpretation of the specification, in the sense of additional authors and ideas, which you don't necessarily need to adopt or follow. They have overlaid an additional discussion of philosophers and philosophical ideas in order to evaluate the fairly brief content of the specification. So it is essential you understand that you will be examined on knowledge and content alone - and you can use whoever you like to evaluate and criticise this content.

You should download and print out now a hard copy of the relevant pages of the specification.

- The three papers need to be integrated to produce what is called synoptic insight. Here we call them Thought Points. This literally means elements of the three papers that can be 'seen together' or linked up. For example, Kant's moral argument (Philosophy of Religion) links and to his ethics which links to John Hick's universal pluralism (Christian Thought H573/3) as Hick is greatly inspired by Kant. The Peped website shows additional ways to integrate the three papers and there will be a revision section accessible for those who have this workbook showing you how to increase your synoptic understanding.

Those who have this integrated workbook should have a head-start, but you need to supplement it with other ideas and sample answers.

- Our approach is to teach for structures of thought. These are given by the mind-maps in this workbook. Notice these are not prescriptive - you can make up your own if you wish, or amend these. But to write effective philosophical essays, you need to write according to structures of thought and not some formula for essay-writing (which you may find online). These structures are the same you will find on the peped website and in our revision guides.

- Our aim here is to help you ask the right questions, in the right order, to help you teach yourself. The workbook does not provide all the answers. This is because we want you to do your own research (using the peped site or the wider internet resources, such as the excellent Internet Encylopaedia of Philosophy). We will also mark your essays for you if you buy an essay-marking credit, or provide a tutor for you in cyberspace who will provide Skype or phone support and guidance.

What is Ethics?

The Meaning of the Word

'Ethics' is from the Greek 'ethikos' or 'ethos' meaning 'character'.

Socrates asked "how then should we live?' Or what norms (values) should I live by?

Moral philosophy according to Bernard Williams is not just about principles, but about arguments:

"A style of argument that claims to be rationally persuasive." Williams, Bernard. Ethics and the Limits of Philosophy. p. 2

Exercise 1.1 Fill in the gaps below.

Ethics (from the Greek..........) is the study of how............are derived and applied to specific situations. There are three branches: ....ethics, applied ethics and meta-ethics.

The approach to analysing and evaluating ethics produces an acronym **DARM**.

Derivation of Norms (D)

In this ethics course we look at three elements of ethics:

1. Normative ethics

2. Applied ethics

3. Meta-ethics

How is the norm (value of right and wrong) derived in **normative** ethics? **(D)**

FH Bradley "A moral judgement must be true or false, and its truth or falsehood cannot lie in itself. **They involve a reference to a something beyond,** and this, about which or of which we judge, if it is not fact, what else can it be?" (1883:41)

The question is: what is this 'something beyond" that we point to as some kind of fact in the world which we label as 'good'?

There are really only two routes of reasoning – **a priori** by a deductive method, as Kant uses. Kant takes an imaginative step away from the situation and tries to universalise a general maxim (moral principle). The **ontological argument** in Philosophy of Religion also applies a similar deductive method.

"The Moral law **within**" is what produces wonder in Kant when he discovers it for himself by an internal process of reason and imagination.

A posteriori – by experience, or from experience is the second method of reasoning. Utilitarians and Situation Ethicists argue from our experience of pleasure/happiness, or love.

Of course, we could use two further routes which don't involve reasoning:

1. Follow a command of God blindly.

2. Follow a non-reasoned **intuition** (intuitionism).

3. We could do a combination of these – so follow an intuition (or divine command) until it seemed unreasonable.

Application of the Norm (A)

Applied ethics looks at how norms are applied in real life situations. We need case studies to try to tease out this complexity.

In **euthanasia** cases, when does the unwarranted suffering of an individual become a moral factor to consider?

In **business ethics**, when should a whistleblower 'blow the whistle' on malpractice, corruption or exploitation?

In **sexual ethics**, when is it acceptable to sleep with someone you've just met?

We need to keep this question in mind – what do we do when two moral 'goods' conflict"?

Exercise 1.2: try to write your own example below of a situation where two moral goods conflict. Think perhaps of an example of where you find a close colleague doing something dishonest.

Realism (R) and What it Means to be Human

How realistic is our theory which produces norms (values of good and bad)? Is it true to our understanding of human nature? Moral actions have the following characteristics:

Motive -> Nature of the action -> Consequences -> Feelings

Utilitarians say nothing about **motive** (it's a consequentialist theory) - what matters are the results or consequences of our actions.

Kantians discount **feelings** which have no moral worth – only the motive of the 'good will' is relevant - that is the will which acts out of concern for the moral good alone.

Natural law theorists have an **element** of all these –as we shall see, yet Catholic encyclicals (circulated letters from the Pope) claim the applications such as 'no contraception' are 'inviolable' - they are absolute, unbreakable norms.

Does this make Natural Law 'superior"? Not necessarily. It can still be hard to apply natural law principles in cases of conflict, where two norms are in conflict and we can't keep both at the same time, and it begs the question 'what's the place of conscience"?

All moral theories have to solve the problem of moral conflict. When Corrie Ten Boom told the Gestapo officer in 1942 that she wasn't hiding Jewish people in a cupboard in her bedroom, she was telling a lie. But she told a lie because a **greater good was in conflict** with it: to tell the truth would mean the death of her friends.

Motivation (M)

Why be moral at all? Why not just be selfish? The answer comes in four forms:

1. Morality **benefits** everyone – a self-interested reason.

2. We can be **idealistic** and committed to a higher end – such as building a better world (utilitarianism) or Kant's summum bonum (the greatest good).

3. We feel **sympathy** for others (Mill and Hume's reason to be moral). Hume thought feelings of sympathy were the basis of morality.

4. We **love God** and want to please Him. "If you love me you will obey my commandments", said Jesus.

Exercise 1.3: Self-test – What does **DARM** stand for?

Meta-ethics (Beyond Ethics)

Meta-ethics has two primary concerns.

1. To explore the **foundation** of ethics and to ask whether it exists in the natural world (naturalism) or not.

2. To find out whether it's **meaningful** to say "stealing is wrong' or 'generosity is good'.

This is sometimes expressed as 'discovering whether moral statements are **truth-apt**'. Truth-apt means 'testable against some objective measurement'.

Imagine the following scenario. I am walking in the park and I see a dead body under a tree. I go across and notice blood on the body. I shout out, "Murder, how awful!". The philosopher A.J. Ayer argues I am adding nothing factual to the scene – just an emotive interpretation. Ayer is the originator of a theory we will study later called **emotivism**.

So Ayer argues there is no such thing as a '**moral** fact'. But this view is hotly debated. Most moral theories are both cognitive (making truth claims) and naturalistic (grounded in the natural world and so pointing beyond the action to a fact).

Essay-writing Skill

Exercise 1.4: "Meta-ethics is more useful than Normative ethics'. Discuss.

Write a thesis statement which sums up your one sentence 'line' on this question, using the word 'because'.

Example: "Utilitarianism is more useful than Kantian ethics in solving moral dilemmas".

Thesis statement: "Utilitarianism is more useful than Kantian ethics because it takes into account our feelings of pleasure and pain, and has greater flexibility due to the absence of hard, absolute rules".

Deontological & Teleological

The Meaning of Deon and Telos

Deon means 'duty' in Greek

Telos means 'purpose' in Greek

Natural Law has both deontological and teleological aspects – the 'law' part gives us duties, the word telos comes from the Greek idea that there is a final cause or true purpose for everything. Aristotle taught that the ultimate purpose is **eudaimonia;** the flourishing, fulfilled life. The Natural Law theorist Thomas Aquinas (1225 - 1274) argues for the same goal eudaimonia or (he uses a Latin word) **beatitudo** (blessedness).

Kantian Ethics is deontological because Kant derives duties from a process of **a priori** reasoning - reasoning in the abstract taking a process fo the imagination. These duties he calls categorically and they are **absolute**, unbreakable moral obligations.

Utilitarianism and Situation Ethics are teleological as they point to 'something beyond' (FH Bradley, full quote on page 3) - that 'something' is happiness or pleasure (utilitarians) or agape love (Situation Ethics).

Rules – Hard or Soft?

Kantian deontology has hard rules or **categoricals**. These cannot be broken. They are absolute rules.

Natural Law deontology, as Aquinas teaches it, creates **soft rules** or secondary precepts. These are 'approximate conclusions of reason' says Aquinas. They can be broken, so we can call these rules 'soft', for example, when two moral goods conflict you choose one and follow a right intention.

Mill's **weak rule utilitarianism** also has soft rules, that's what the word 'weak' means in the later ascription of Weak Rule Utilitarianism (Mill never uses this term himself, it was invented by J.O. Urmson in 1953). When two moral goods conflict you revert to being an Act Utilitarian and assess the consequences using your **judgement**.

A Teleological Aspect to all Ethical Theories

There is a teleological aspect to all moral theories, even Kant's. Kant calls this ultimate end the **summum bonum** or greatest good.

But the difference is this: Kant doesn't define goodness by the end (unlike utilitarians).

The summum bonum is a by-product (a result) of the 'good will' according to Kant. Goodness is defined by a rational principle of universalisability – a process of **a priori reason** not an end.

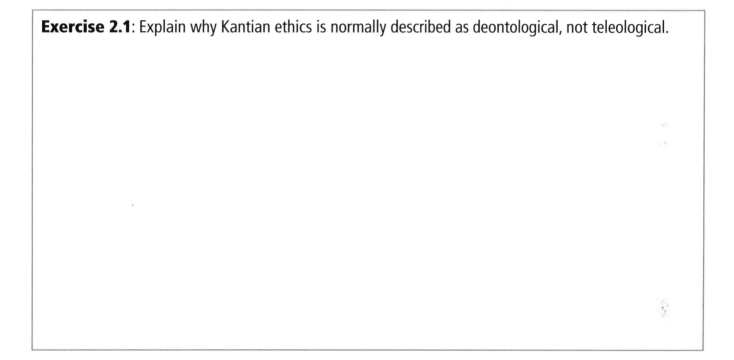

Exercise 2.1: Explain why Kantian ethics is normally described as deontological, not teleological.

Judgement is Involved in all Theories

We all need moral judgement, but it different philosophers argue it comes in different ways.

Kant argues we gain judgment by a process of universalising our behaviour. We practise an a priori process and we get better at it as we involve our minds in the decision.

Mill argues we bring **sympathy** to bear on experiences and consider others and then make a calculation: which action promotes maximum happiness (we need a judgement of what makes ourselves and others happy) and minimum pain.

To a Natural Law theorist we need right judgment to move from the general moral principle (for example, preserve human life) to the specific application (euthanasia is wrong - at least that's the Roman Catholic interpretation which you may or may not accept as valid). The Greek word for this 'right judgement' is **phronesis**, sometimes translated 'practical wisdom'.

Of course, consequentialist judgements can be tricky. We can never be entirely sure we have thought of everything. It seems to involve a God-like knowledge of the future.

Back to Bernard Williams' quote in the last chapter – moral philosophy is about bringing our **rational judgement** to bear on events and actions.

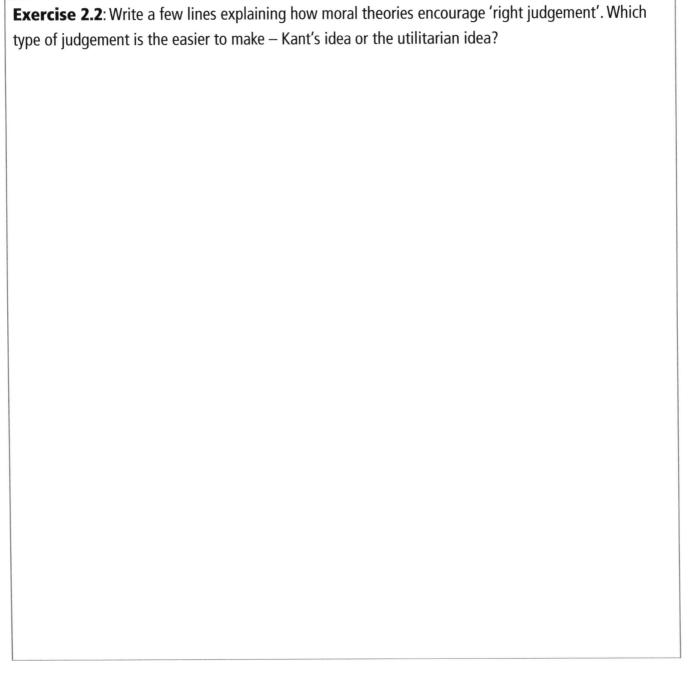

Exercise 2.2: Write a few lines explaining how moral theories encourage 'right judgement'. Which type of judgement is the easier to make – Kant's idea or the utilitarian idea?

Situation Ethics - Teleological Ethics

"The means justifies the end. Nothing else". Joseph Fletcher

Background

"Situation ethics" was a term Joseph Fletcher (1905-1991) adopted in 1966. Fletcher was an Episcopalian (American Anglican) priest, so this theory may be described as a Christian ethic (a form of Christian relativism, or liberal Christian morality).

It is also reflected in the life of the German martyr Dietrich Bonhoeffer, who rejected the absolute "thou shalt not kill" in order to participate in the Stauffenberg bomb plot of 1944, and the teachings of German theologians such as Emil Brunner.

Situation ethics takes normative principles – like natural law precepts or Kant's categorical imperative – and generalises them so that we can "make sense" of our experience when facing moral dilemmas.

But situation ethics rejects any attempt to turn these generalisations into firm rules and laws, what Fletcher (1966) called a form of "ethical idolatry."

For situationists, love is the supreme principle, as John Lennon and Paul McCartney put it in the Beatles' 1960s song, "All you need is love."

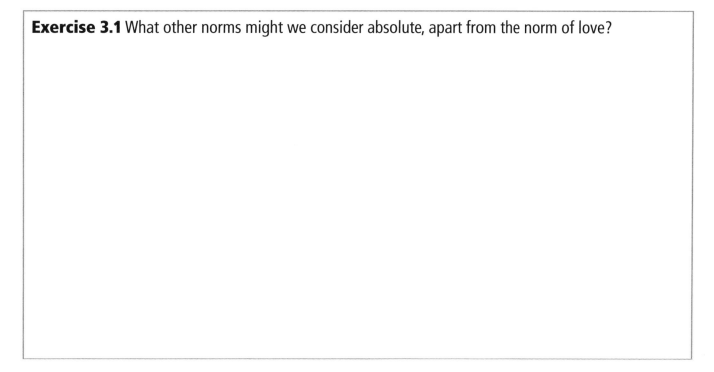

Exercise 3.1 What other norms might we consider absolute, apart from the norm of love?

What does the Cartoon Suggest?

Fundamental Good - Agape

Love is concerned with our neighbour's good. Agape is the highest form of love - a sacrificial, attitudinal, committed, impartial form of love that puts the interests of friend and stranger first.

The Parable of the Good Samaritan is the New Testament explanation of this form of neighbourly love. **(Luke 10:25-37)**

Exercise 3.2 Read the Parable of the Good Samaritan (**Luke 10:25-37**). To what extent do you think Jesus is espousing situationism? Clue: think about the final saying 'go and do likewise' which might mean 'go and do this kind of thing in this sort of situation'.

Antinomianism and Legalism

Joseph Fletcher argues that situation ethics lies between **antinomianism** (no law) and **legalism** (slavishly following law without using your judgement).

This approach Fletcher calls **positivism** – we accept this 'good' by faith and then act on it. There remains one supreme principle - love.

Exercise 3.3: Situation Ethics lies between antinomianism and legalism. Explain this idea in Fletcher's Situation Ethics in one sentence.

How Relativistic?

Is Situation Ethics pure relativism? Richard Jacobs explains how it is best described by Fletcher's own term 'principled relativism'.

What the situationists seek to avoid is the charge that they are ethical relativists at the level of norms. Situationists rightly point out that normative principles depend on a number of factors unique to particular instances. Thus, situationists conclude, normative principles - although helpful for understanding what ethics requires- do not transcend all situations as normative ethicists would like. For example, there are many situations in which we may understand clearly that lying, adultery, murder, and theft are unethical as principles but we may also understand with equal clarity that these prohibitions may not apply given the idiosyncratic circumstances in which we find ourselves. It is in this sense situation ethics is better called "principled relativism." (Richard Jacobs, Villanova University)

Exercise 3.4: Explain how Situation Ethics is best described as 'principled relativism'.

Four Working Principles

Positivism

"Positivism" here is not the same as 'logical positivism' in meta-ethics. Fletcher means something different:

Any moral or value judgment in ethics, like a theologian's faith propositions, is a decision — not a conclusion. It is a choice, not a result reached by force of logic. (1966:47)

Fletcher says that he **cannot prove** that the only law is the law of love: it is not a result of logic or reasoning, rather it is a decision we take, it is like the "theologian's faith".

Personalism

We maximise love by considering the person in a situation — the "who" of a situation. Fletcher says:

Love is of people, by people, and for people. Things are to be used; people are to be loved… Loving actions are the only conduct permissible. (1966:51)

Pragmatism

"Pragmatism" is a very specific philosophical position adopted by **John Dewey** (1859–1952), and **William James** (1842–1910). Fletcher does not want his theory associated with this meaning of pragmatism.

Pragmatism means we do not try to work out what to do in the abstract (as with Kant's Categorical Imperative), but rather we explore how moral views might play out in each real life situations, case by case.

Relativism

If situations vary then consequences won't be the same, and what we ought to do (what is morally 'right') will change. There remains one absolute - **agape** love - and everything is made relative to this.

"Love relativises the absolute, it does not absolutise the relative". Fletcher

---

Exercise 3.5: What does Fletcher mean by the quote above? Try putting it into your own words.

The Place of Conscience

Fletcher sees "conscience" as a **verb** and not a noun.

Conscience is not the name of an internal faculty (as in Natural Law theory) nor is it a sort of internal "moral compass" and so 'not a noun'. For example, conscience is sometimes seen as a 'voice of God' within us, acting upon us.

Fletcher argues conscience is a **verb**.

Imagine we have heard some bullies laughing because they have sent our friend some offensive texts and we are trying to decide whether or not to check his phone to delete the texts before he does. The old "noun" view of conscience would get us to think about this in the abstract, perhaps reason about it, or ask for guidance from the Holy Spirit.

According to Fletcher this is wrong. Instead, we need to be in the situation, and experience the situation, we need to be doing (hence it is a "verb") the experiencing. Maybe, we might conclude that it is right to go into our friend's phone, maybe we will not, but whatever happens the outcome could not have been known beforehand. What our conscience would have us do is revealed when we live in the world and not through armchair reflection. (source: Dummock and Fisher)

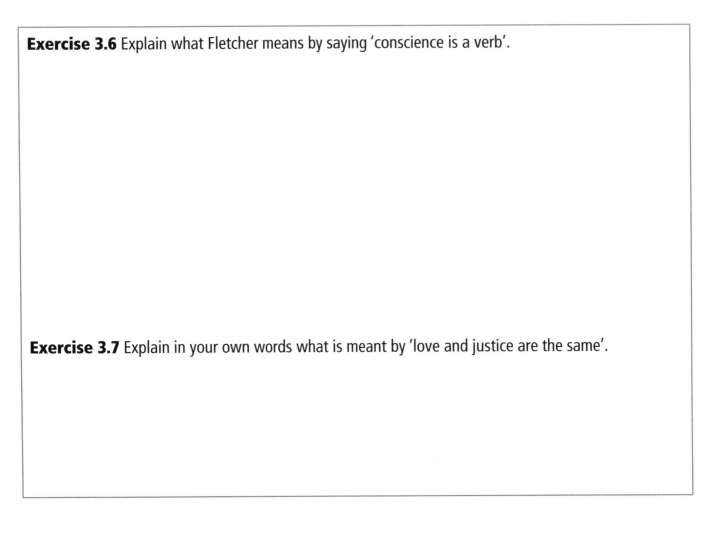

Exercise 3.6 Explain what Fletcher means by saying 'conscience is a verb'.

Exercise 3.7 Explain in your own words what is meant by 'love and justice are the same'.

Six Fundamental Principles

Love only is always good 'Only one 'thing' is intrinsically good; namely, love: nothing else at all'	Love is intrinsically valuable, it has internet worth. Love is good. Nothing else has intrinsic value but 'it gains or acquires its value only because it happens to help persons (thus being good) or to hurt persons (thus being bad)'. A lie is not intrinsically wrong. It is wrong if it harms people, but may sometimes be right. *'For the Situationist, what makes the lie right is its loving purpose; [they are] not hypnotised by some abstract law, 'Thou shalt not lie'.'*
Love is the only norm (rule) 'The ruling norm of Christian decision is love: nothing else'	Love replaces the law. The law should only be obeyed in the interests of love, not for the law's sake! Fletcher rejects Natural Law. He says 'There are no [natural] universal laws held by all men everywhere at all times.' *Jesus summarized the entire law by saying 'Love God' and 'Love your neighbour'.* Love is the only law. The problem with this is that it allows the individual to do anything in the name of love - there are no rules to say that someone has done the wrong thing.
Love and justice are the same 'Love and justice are the same, for justice is love distributed, nothing else.'	There can be no love without justice. Consider any injustice - a child starving, a man arrested without charge etc. These are examples of a lack of love. If love was properly shared out, there would be no injustice.
Love is not liking 'Love wills the neighbour's good whether we like him or not.'	Love is discerning and critical, not sentimental. Martin Luther King described Agape love as a 'creative, redemptive goodwill to all men'. He said it would be nonsense to ask people to like their violent oppressors. Christian love is a non-selfish love of all people.
Love justifies the means 'Only the end justifies the means; nothing else,'	When someone said to Fletcher 'The end doesn't justify the means', he said 'Then what on earth does?'. If an action causes harm, it is wrong. If good comes of it, it is right. Fletcher says you can't claim to be right by following a rule (like 'Do not lie') knowing it will cause great harm. Only the end or outcome can justify your action.
Love decides there and then	There are no rules about what should or shouldn't be done - in each situation, you decide there and then what the cost loving thing to do is.

The Means/Ends Problem in Ethics

One of the most important debates in ethics concerns the question of whether the **end** justifies the **means**.

Consider President Harry Truman's decision in 1945 to drop two atom bombs on Japan cities of Hiroshima and Nagasaki. He knew hundreds of thousands of innocent civilians would die.

He also knew many US and allied service personnel would die taking Japan, many Japanese civilians in US conventional bombing, and that Emperor Hirohito had ordered the killing of all US prisoners of war if an enemy foot stepped on Japanese soil.

I realise the tragic significance of the atomic bomb. Its production and its use were not lightly undertaken by this Government. But we knew that our enemies were on the search for it. We know now how close they were to finding it. And we knew the disaster, which would come to this Nation, and to all peace-loving nations, to all civilisation, if they had found it first. That is why we felt compelled to undertake the long and uncertain and costly labor of discovery and production.

We won the race of discovery against the Germans. Having found the bomb we have used it. We have used it against those who attacked us without warning at Pearl Harbour, against those who have starved and beaten and executed American prisoners of war, against those who have abandoned all pretence of obeying international laws of warfare. We have used it in order to shorten the agony of war, in order to save the lives of thousands and thousands of young Americans. (President Harry Truman)

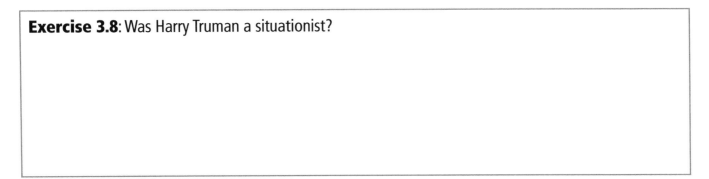

Exercise 3.8: Was Harry Truman a situationist?

Note: Estimates for US casualties were as high as 500,000. But suppose the out-turn had been 20,000 US dead. Would it still have been morally justified to kill 325,000 innocent civilians?

Is this a form of racism – a Japanese life is worth less than a US life?

Hard Cases in Ethics

Fletcher dislikes legalism because it cannot handle hard cases (where two moral goods come into conflict, as with Corrie Ten Boom hiding Jewish friends in a secret cupboard in 1942). The OCR syllabus requires us to apply situation ethics to euthanasia cases and address 'the issues surrounding euthanasia'.

Euthanasia

A terminally ill patient wants to die; what ought we to do? Fletcher founded the American euthanasia society so we can guess his position. The key issue is: what does, and does not, get considered in "the situation", and does it depend on what we already think is important. Do we consider his religious views, the fact that he has three children whom depend on him or the **implications for society** generally? What about the type of illness, the type of death, who he leaves behind, the effect it might have on the judicial system, the effect on the medical profession and the effect on other elderly people as euthanasia is legalised.

Fletcher advises us to "ask what will bring about the most love in the situation". Yet one person might see the situation in one way and someone else see it in another.

What weight do we place on the effect on relatives of euthanasia versus the wishes of the person involved?

Exercise 3.5: Euthanasia - an example

Your parent is lying very sick in bed. They have no prospect of recovery and the pain-killers don't seem to be working. Moreover, you will inherit £1 million if they die now, but if they stay alive it's possible they may alter their will and disinherit you after a recent argument. You decide to convince them the time has come to choose euthanasia.

Write a paragraph discussing this question: is this the most loving outcome?

Research the Starmer Guidelines issued in 2012 by then Solicitor-Geenral Keir Starmer to help police decide whether to charge those who assist a person to die (a crime, according to the Suicide Act 1966)

Name two guidelines which are broken in the case above. https://www.theguardian.com/society/2009/sep/23/assisted-suicide-guidelines-legal

Thought Points

1. Was Dietrich Bonhoeffer a situationist? (OCR Christian Thought paper, section 5)

2. Is situation ethics the same as utilitarian ethics? People sometimes suggest this. But Mill would disagree. We all pursue happiness/pleasure, says Mill, but we can see few of us pursue agape love. Secondly, Mill argues for the social setting of justice – the rules and principles embedded in law which guarantee a happier society because we won't be arbitrarily arrested. This is very different from a situationist calculation of justice in an individual decision. Mill elevates rules : Fletcher seems to play down rules. William Barclay makes the same point (Ethics in a Permissive Society).

Some Confusions to Avoid

1. Fletcher has his own use of **positivism**, meaning 'expressing a faith position'. Normally positivism means 'testable by evidence'.

2. Fletcher has is own meaning of **pragmatism**. Normally 'pragmatic' is opposed to 'principled'. But Fletcher means 'a case by case, situational approach'.

3. Fletcher has his own meaning of **relativism**. When Pope Benedict talked about the 'tyranny of relativism', he was meaning something like 'an attitude where anything goes'. But Fletcher means 'everything is relative to the principle of agape and the consequences of the action in maximising agape'.

4. Situation ethics is not 'highly subjective'. Fletcher denies this: it's not about our individual feelings but an objective measure of the maximising of love, with everyone affected included. Agape itself is an attitude, not a feeling. perhaps the judgment is subjective - but this applies to all ethical theories.

Nonetheless, there is a **subjective judgement** to be made. For example, Fletcher supports euthanasia and even argued that starvation victims should be allowed to die. We might strongly disagree with him - after all 'love and justice are the same'. What does justice mean here?

Essay-writing

"An individual ought to have complete autonomy over a decision to end their own life". Discuss with reference to situation ethics.

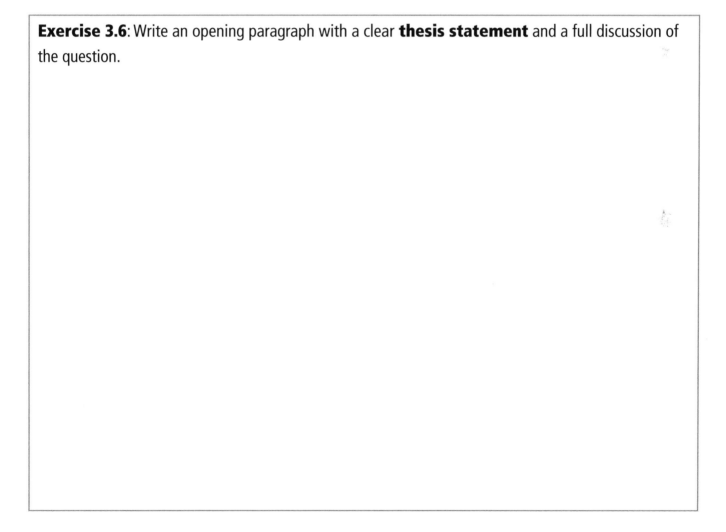

Exercise 3.6: Write an opening paragraph with a clear **thesis statement** and a full discussion of the question.

Example: "Situation ethics is the most useful way of solving moral dilemmas". Discuss

Answer: Situation ethics takes a pragmatic, case by case approach to moral decisions which should be taken with an eye on the most loving outcome as a primary goal. In this essay I take an example from the euthanasia debate to demonstrate how situation ethics suffers three main difficulties: we do not know what all the consequences will be, we have difficulty applying the supreme value of agape love, and as Barclay and Mill would both agree, we cannot abandon rules so easily if we are to build the happy life within a happy society. Therefore it isn't the most useful way and natural law ethics is superior on all three of these issues.

Bentham's Act Utilitarianism - Teleological Ethics

Background

Jeremy Bentham (1748-1832) was a friend of Mill's father, James Mill. Although utilitarianism really goes back to Greek thinkers like Epicurus, it was developed and made fashionable by Bentham and James Mill's son John Stuart Mill who harnessed it to the cause of social reform. The utilitarians disliked both natural law theorists (who justified undemocratic hierarchies) and intuitionists (who claimed some divinely inspired intuition that some people were less equal than others.

One Intrinsic Good

Bentham argues there is '**one intrinsic good**'- pleasure. Intrinsic goods cannot be proven, and the argument here is there is as a psychological fact something which everyone desires - our own pleasure, and a moral bad we avoid - our own pain. This operates as a **psychological assumption** (how would you prove it without asking everyone, which is impossible?).

Exercise 4.1: Explain in one sentence what is meant by an 'intrinsic good".

Bentham's Structure of Thought

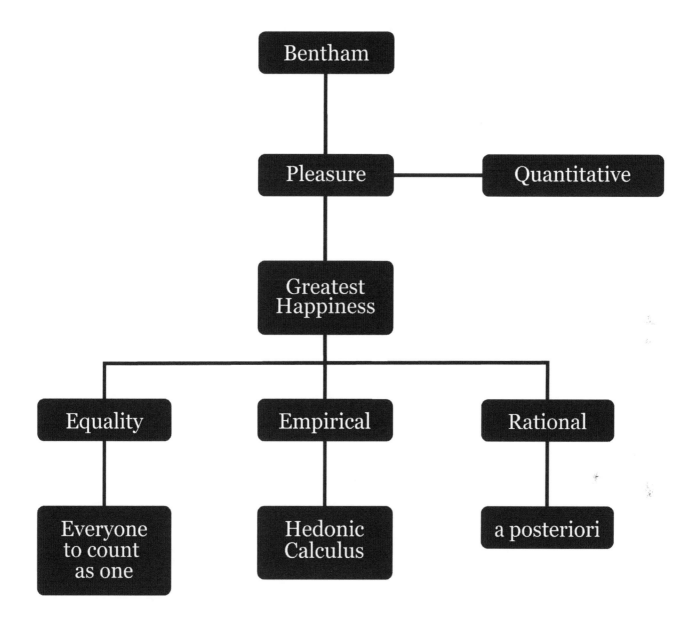

Pleasure is Quantitive

Bentham argues 'pushpin is as good as poetry'. What does he mean by this? Pushpin is a pub game of the eighteenth century and Bentham believed that all pleasures of whatever kind were of equal value.

The utility of all these arts and sciences,—I speak both of those of amusement and curiosity,—the value which they possess, is exactly in proportion to the pleasure they yield. Every other species of pre-eminence which may be attempted to be established among them is altogether fanciful. Prejudice apart, the game of push-pin is of equal value with the arts and sciences of music and poetry. If the game of push-pin furnish more pleasure, it is more valuable than either. Everybody can play at push-pin: poetry and music are relished only by a few. The game of push-pin is always innocent: it were well could the same be always asserted of poetry. Indeed, between poetry and truth there is natural opposition: false morals and fictitious nature. The poet always stands in need of something false. When he pretends to lay his foundations in truth, the ornaments of his superstructure are fictions; his business consist in stimulating our passions, and exciting our prejudices. Truth, exactitude of every kind is fatal to poetry. The poet must see everything through coloured media, and strive to make every one else do the same. It is true, there have been noble spirits, to whom poetry and philosophy have been equally indebted; but these exceptions do not counteract the mischiefs which have resulted from this magic art. If poetry and music deserve to he preferred before a game of push-pin, it must be because they are calculated to gratify those individuals who are most difficult to be pleased. (Bentham, Rationale of Reward, Book 3 Chapter 1)

Exercise 4.2: Write your own example from your experience that brings out the same point, that pushpin and poetry are of equal value.

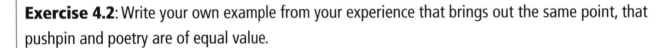

An Empirical Philosophy

Bentham was trying to bring science to moral philosophy by arguing we could calculate a good moral outcome. He came up with a way of measuring pleasure by seven criteria, called the hedonic calculus.

How does the hedonic calculus do this?

Bentham believed that pleasures were empirically measurable by a hedonic calculus. This calculus had seven dimensions which give the utility calculation a value in some measure (shall we call them utils?).

In estimating a pleasure by itself, Bentham asks us to consider four dimensions.

- **INTENSITY** - how strong is the pleasure?

- **DURATION** - how long does it last?

- **CERTAINTY** - how sure is the pleasure?

- **PROPINQUITY** - how near is it, or how soon will I experience it?

Henry Sidgwick (1838-1900)criticises Bentham for placing such a value on propinquity. For the more distant a pleasure, the more uncertain may be its occurrence.

"Proximity is a property of pleasures and pains which it is reasonable to disregard except in so far as it diminishes uncertainty. For my feelings a year hence should be just as important to me as my feelings next minute, if only I could make an equally sure forecast of them. Indeed this equal and impartial concern for all parts of one's conscious life is perhaps the most prominent element in the common notion of the rational – as opposed to the merely impulsive – pursuit of pleasure" (Methods of Ethics 124n; cf. 111).

Then Bentham asks us to consider whether the pleasure will lead on to further pleasures and suggests two more dimensions. These two result from actions.

- **FECUNDITY** - how many more pleasures will result?

- **PURITY** - are there any negative pains attached to the pleasure?

Then Bentham applies these to the wider group:

- **EXTENT** - how many more people are affected?

This produces the principle : act in such a way that your actions produce the greatest amount of pleasure and the least amount of pain.

However, a problem emerges which worried later utilitarians like Henry Sidgwick. Where this principle provides a motivation for my action, why should I care about the happiness of others? It is not clear why I should want to maximise the happiness of a stranger I'd never met, rather than just my family and friends. Moreover, do we need this complex list of seven dimensions?

David Brink suggests:

"The whole taxonomy seems unnecessarily complex. Because the utilitarian asks us to maximize value, he has to be able to make sense of quantities or magnitudes of value or pleasure associated with different options, where pleasure increases the value of an option and pain decreases the value of the option. Intensity and duration are really the only two variables". (David Brink)

Suppose as a teacher I discover a colleague leaking exam questions to his students. If I blow the whistle and expose the fraud, my own career could be in ruins as I may be blacklisted by the school and other schools for rocking the boat. Moreover, my colleague's career will be ruined and his students will do less well and so their happiness will be less. So as an action it seems to be the right thing to keep quiet.

But the general happiness of society, including those students who will just fail to get in to the university of their choice because his students have done better than they should, seems to demand that I speak out. But why should I care about the wider society? After all, I will never meet them, whereas I will meet those gaining from the act of cheating every day.

It is hard to see how utilitarians would ever be whistle blowers in business ethics.

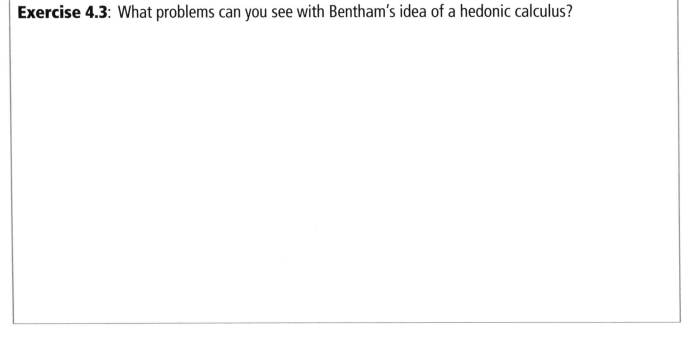

Exercise 4.3: What problems can you see with Bentham's idea of a hedonic calculus?

Thought-points

1. David Hume was the father of utilitarianism because he argued feelings of **sympathy** are the foundation of morality. "Reason is the slave of the passions", he said.

2. Paradoxically, utilitarians are **naturalists**, whereas in meta-ethics Hume is also the father of logical positivism – the view that ethical language is **non-naturalistic** and so meaningless in factual terms, and cannot be derived a priori either (Kant's way of deriving norms).

3. "Utilitarians are **relativists**". There are three meanings of relativism: subjective (up to me), consequentialist (linked to results) and particular to culture. So 'relativism' needs interpreting.

> **Exercise 4.4**: Explain how utilitarians are **absolutist** in one of the three meanings, (objective, non-conequentialist, universal) but **relativist** in another of the three meanings of relativism.

The Pleasure Machine

Robert Nozick's pleasure machine envisages us wired up to a pleasure machine with a key board. We can have any quantity of any pleasure we like. An issue, for example, in sexual ethics is whether lifelike robot sex-toys are morally abhorrent. JCC Smart comments:

This calls up a pleasant picture of the voluptuary of the future, a bald-headed man with a number of electrodes protruding from his skull, one to give the physical pleasure of sex, one for eating, one for drinking, and so on. Now is this the sort of life our ethical planning should culminate in? (JCC Smart 1994:19).

Essay-writing Skill

We need to practise weaving AO2 evaluation in with analysis. Never tack evaluation on to the end of an essay.

Example: "Bentham's philosophy is swinish (the philosophy of a pig)". Discuss

Exercise 4.5: Write a couple of sentences explaining the evaluative idea of 'swinish' in the above question.

Example: "Bentham's philosophy is pseudo-science". Discuss

Answer: Bentham believed you could bring science to bear on moral questions of right and wrong. There was one intrinsic good, a thing good in itself, which he posits rather than proves. This good is pleasure. It makes no matter whether it is bodily, intellectual, spiritual or sensual. According to Bentham we can calculate it from a hedonic calculus, then add up some units of pleasure or happiness so produced. However, his method is indeed pseudo-science because it is impractical and impossible to calculate by this seven-fold criteria for assessing pleasure. We will never know whether my util equals your util – it is simply too subjective.

Evaluation Points on Bentham

1. Pleasure is the one intrinsic good. Is it? What about duty (Kant) or purpose (Natural Law)?

2. Happiness is not an end in itself but the result (by-product) of pursuing other goals. Do you agree?

3. Only God can accurately predict consequences. Is this fatal to Bentham's consequentialist ethics?

4. Bentham ignores the role of character in living the fulfilled life. This is Mill's criticism of Bentham's version in Mill's Essay on Bentham. Do you agree?

Afterword

Although there is more we might say about Bentham, two crucial criticisms remain: that it is just passive pleasure which we may be maximised (as in Nozick's pleasure machine) and secondly, I can be sacrificed for the greater happiness of everyone.

Mill's Weak Rule Utilitarianism -Teleological Ethics

Background

John Stuart Mill (1806-1873) is famous for his views on social reform, the liberation of women, and for his essays on Utilitarianism and On Liberty. In his essay On Liberty he introduces the 'harm principle': "the only reason to restrict the liberty of the individual is to prevent harm to others". In Utilitarianism he attempts to answer critics of the time like Thomas Carlyle and novelist Charles Dickens. Mill is keen to stress the social context of happiness and the importance of a safe and just society.

J.O. Urmson (1952)

J.O. Urmson introduced the classification of Mill's utilitarianism as 'weak rule utilitarianism' in 1952 – Mill never uses it himself. But it sums up quite well how Mill argues we should generally follow social rules that past experience shows maximises happiness, but break those rules in cases of moral dilemmas where happiness is best served.

Thought point: some have argued rule utilitarianism collapses into act utilitarianism. Do you agree?

Mill disliked three things about Bentham's Theory:

- Quantitative pleasure is swinish (problem of being passive and self-indulgent)

- Risks sacrificing an individual for general happiness (problem of injustice)

- Social utility – background of rules was neglected (problem of the lack of social context)

"Bentham's theory demonstrates the deficiencies of a system of ethics which does not pretend to aid individuals in the formation of their own character". (JS Mill, Essay on Bentham)

Mill's Structure of Thought

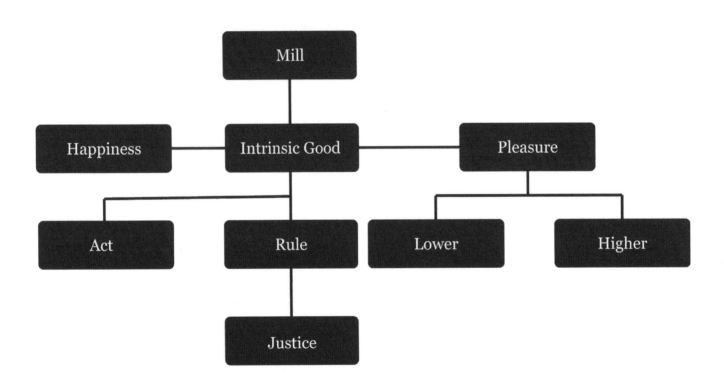

Important Points

1. Mill is **inconsistent** in his essay. Are we focusing on pleasure or happiness? He begins his essay by arguing 'there is one intrinsic good, pleasure'. He then says half way through "happiness consists in many and various pleasures, few and transitory pains, and a predominance of the active over the passive, not expecting more from life than it is capable of delivering". He adds activity and life-time goals, and then in his final chapter, principles of justice.

2. He seems to end up closer to Aristotle's view of **eudaimonia**, the flourishing life lived in the context of the moral, just society. Moreover, he seems critical of Bentham's 'swinish' philosophy.

3. His version of rule utilitarianism combines rules of thumb or soft rules (which can be broken) with act utilitarianism (when there's moral dilemma where two goods conflict, we will need to use our **judgement**). It has both act and rule utilitarian elements.

Mill's Analogy of the Navigator

"Nobody argues that the art of navigation is not founded on astronomy, because sailors cannot wait to calculate the Nautical Almanack. Being rational creatures, they go to sea with it ready calculated; and all rational creatures go out upon the sea of life with their minds made up on the common questions of right and wrong. Whatever we adopt as the fundamental principle of morality, we require subordinate principles to apply it by; the impossibility of doing without them, being common to all systems, can afford no argument against any one in particular; but gravely to argue as if no such secondary principles could be had, and as if mankind had remained till now, and always must remain, without drawing any general conclusions from the experience of human life, is as high a pitch, I think, as absurdity has ever reached in philosophical controversy". *(Utilitarianism, II).*

Exercise 5.1: Explain how Mill's own analogy of the navigator can be used to explain Mill's weak rule utilitarianism.

Higher and Lower Pleasures

Mill appeals to the "superior being" who has experienced both higher and lower pleasures

"A sense of dignity, which all human beings possess in one form or other, and in some, though by no means in exact, proportion to their higher faculties, and which is so essential a part of the happiness of those in whom it is strong that nothing which conflicts with it could be otherwise than momentarily an object of desire to them. Whoever supposes that this preference takes place at a sacrifice of happiness – that the superior being, in anything like equal circumstances, is not happier than the inferior – confounds the two very different ideas of happiness", (II.5).

Exercise 5.2: Is this distinction of higher and lower pleasures just snobbery? Research the role of character in Mill's ethics

http://peped.org/philosophicalinvestigations/extract-10-mill-on-the-importance-of-character/

Justice

Mill takes trouble to argue in the last section of his essay on Utilitarianism that unhappiness is caused by selfishness, by people "acting only for themselves", and that for a person to be happy they need "to cultivate a fellow feeling with the collective interests of mankind" and "in the golden rule of Jesus we find the whole ethics of utility".

We might add that the Situation Ethicist Joseph Fletcher claims Jesus as his own, as does Immanuel Kant who argued that Matthew 7:23 "do to others as you would have them do to you" was very close to his first formulation of the categorical imperative, that of universalisability.

Perhaps Mill recognised that utilitarian philosophy contradicted the argument in his, in my view, much greater essay On Liberty, where he argues that the only justification for infringing personal liberty is to prevent harm to others (the **Harm Principle**). So the utilitarian argument for locking up thousands of Japanese Americans during the second world war, that some of them might be spies, would have no justification according to Mill's On Liberty.

In Utilitarianism Mill defends the concept of rights in terms of utility: "To have a right, then, is, I conceive, to have something which society should defend me in possession of. If the objector asks why? I can give no other answer than general utility", (Utilitarianism, Chapter V).

So Mill appears to be arguing here that general happiness requires that some **rights** be guaranteed, such as the rights to life, liberty, and property. So the rules become: life is sacred and can never be taken away, freedom is a right which can only be infringed under particular circumstances, and property is defended by rules of access and entitlement.

Yet a little later in the essay, Mill appears to argue that these rights can be infringed for the greater good.

"Justice is a name for certain moral requirements, which, regarded collectively, stand higher in the scale of social utility, and are therefore of more paramount obligation, than any others: though particular cases may occur in which some other social duty is so important as to overrule any one of the general maxims of justice. Thus to save a life it may not only be allowable, but a duty, to steal, or take by force, the necessary food or medicine, or to kidnap, or compel to officiate, the only qualified medical practitioner", (Utilitarianism, V).

Mill goes on to stress the importance of rules underpinning the idea of justice, which he has attempted to show are grounded on the greatest happiness principle. These rules, he says, have a "more absolute obligation", implying that in cases of conflicting claims to right action (such as occurred for Jim with the Indians) the rules of justice and implicit rights to life, liberty and property must take precedence.

"I account the justice which is grounded on utility to be the chief part, and incomparably the most sacred and binding part, of all morality. Justice is a name for certain classes of moral rules, which concern the essentials of human well-being more nearly, and are therefore of more absolute obligation, than any other rules for the guidance of life." (Utilitarianism, V)

The objection here is that in arguing for rules Mill applies deontological (duty-based) principles for justification – so the 'not stealing' rule is justified, not because we know that this will maximise utility (which we can't know without evidence), but because it is not rational to have a society in which everyone steals.

Mill counters this objection with a strong social utility argument: only such rules make for a happy (secure, confident, stable) society.

Exercise 5.3: Does Mill's argument for justice and utility overcome the objection that utilitarianism overrides minority rights (the justice problem)?

Williams' Integrity Objection

"A feature of utilitarianism is that it cuts out a kind of consideration which for some others makes a difference to what they feel about such cases: a consideration involving the idea, as we might first and very simply put it, that each of us is specially responsible for what he does, rather than for what other people do. This is an idea closely connected with the value of integrity." (Smart and Williams, 1994)

An important issue in ethics is whether the end justifies the means. In the Jim and the Indians example, you're asked to shoot one Indian to save nineteen. The end (save nineteen) justifies the means (one death). Williams argues we just couldn't do this: we are people of **integrity**.

Exercise 5.4: Research Bernard Williams' example of Jim and the Indians. Can you think of a contemporary example of your own?

Some Quotes to Consider

1. *"For the dictates of utility are neither more nor less than the dictates of the most extensive and enlightened (that is well-advised) benevolence."* Jeremy Bentham

2. *"Utilitarian moralists have gone beyond almost all others in affirming that the motive has nothing to do with the morality of the action, though much with the worth of the agent."*

J.S.Mill

3. *"I find it hard to believe that an action or rule can be right or wrong if there is no good or evil connected with it". William Frankena*

4. *"Bentham's philosophy may be too simplistic and too complicated. It may be too simplistic in that there are values other than pleasure, and it seems too complicated in its artificial hedonic calculus". Louis Pojman*

5. *"Utilitarianism has two virtues...it gives us a clear decision procedure in arriving at our answer about what to do. The second virtue appeals to our sense that morality is made for humans (and other animals?) and that morality is not so much about rules as about helping people and alleviating the suffering of the world". Louis Pojman*

6. *"In the long run, and when reinterpreted by socialists like Robert Owen, utilitarianism in practice did some good, even though it never made much sense as a philosophy. In the short term, it was just one more disaster inflicted upon the British working class." George Lichtheimm*

7. *"I do not care about the greatest good for the greatest number . . . Most people are poop-heads: I do not care about them at all." James Alan Gardener - Ascending.*

8. *"If we British were Utilitarians we would have to believe that imprisoning the innocent and torturing suspects was justified if the Home Secretary thought it a good thing for our peace of mind." William Donaldson*

9. *"The end may justify the means as long as there is something that justifies the end." Leon Trotsky*

Essay-writing Skill: the Five Paragraph Structure

Exercise 5.5: Question "Mill's utilitarianism escapes the difficulties of Bentham's". Discuss

Write an essay plan as a five paragraph structure, like the following example.

Paragraph 1 Thesis statement

Example: Five Paragraph Structure

Answer: "Bentham's philosophy is a pig's philosophy'. Discuss

Thesis: Bentham's philosophy may be described as a pig's philosophy, as Thomas Carlyle did, as it focuses on quantitative pleasure. But this is an overstatement.

Paragraph 2 Development

Bentham argues 'pushpin is as good as poetry'. His idea of pleasure is defined by a hedonic calculation. I prefer football, you prefer Mozart.

Paragraph 3 Development

However, this is a social philosophy because everyone's pleasure needs to be accounted for. We need to invoke Hume's idea of sympathy – understand others. Or ask them.

Paragraph 4 Egalitarianism

Everyone is to count as one. The Queen's hedons count equally to mine. But what if the Queen gets 3,000 hedons out of torturing me? A problem arises.

Paragraph 5 …

Natural Law - Deontological Ethics
Background

Thomas Aquinas (1225-1274) sought to reconcile the works of Aristotle with Biblical Christianity. His greatest work is called Summa Theologica (normally written in references as ST). When the Christian armies reconquered Toledo in Spain in 1085 (under Islamic rule since 711) they found in the libraries of Toledo the works of Aristotle in Aramaic. Aquinas takes the Latin translation of Aristotle's works and moulds the Greek teleological worldview to Christian thought. Aristotle argued that everything has an ultimate purpose (telos) - and the human purpose is to reason well towards the creation of a flourishing life.

Natural Law

Natural Law is a deontological theory within a teleological (Aristotelean, Greek) worldview, based on the exercise of right reason. Aquinas argues:

"The participation of the eternal law in the rational creature is called the natural law."

The **eternal law** is the divine blueprint which we find revealed by scientific enquiry and research. All the laws of mathematics, physics, and the moral law are part of the eternal law.

Aquinas puts it like this:

Now God, by His wisdom, is the Creator of all things in relation to which He stands as the artist to his works of art. Moreover He governs all the acts and movements that are to be found in each single creature. So, as the type of the Divine Wisdom, inasmuch as by Wisdom all things are created, has the character of art; so the type of Divine Wisdom, as moving all things to their due end or proper purpose, bears the character of law. Accordingly the eternal law is nothing else than embodiment of Divine Wisdom. For every knowledge of truth is a kind of reflection and participation of the eternal law. Since then the eternal law is the plan of government in the Chief Governor, all the plans of government in the inferior governors must be derived from the eternal law. But these plans of inferior governors are all other laws besides the eternal law. (Aquinas, ST I-II Q93)

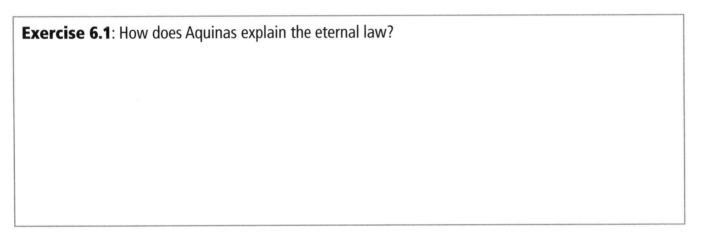

Exercise 6.1: How does Aquinas explain the eternal law?

Thought point: Mary Daly, feminist theologian, talks about the **Quintessence** which is a kind of reality behind all reality. The eternal law is a form of this quintessence.

Humans receive the moral law in two ways, but note, they are only **partial revelations** and we still need to use our reason:

1. The natural law

2. The divine law (the Bible)

There are two ways of Mapping Aquinas' Natural Law

1. Deontological Four Laws

2. Teleological Rational Purpose

Deontological Diamond

Exercise 6.2: Draw a diamond with eternal law at the top, natural law and divine law at the two sides, and human law at the bottom. Eternal law is the blueprint in God's mind which is partially (not perfectly) revealed in natural and divine law. Human law needs to reflect these. (Thought point – you can link this to the teleological design argument in Philosophy of Religion, and also to the debate between Science and Christianity, and whether the two are 'overlapping magisteria' as Stephen Gould suggests, or completely distinct, as Richard Dawkins argues)

Ratio and the Eternal Law

Ratio is a Greek word meaning reason. But it means a special sort of analytical or deductive reason, which takes time and effort to work out, in contrast to intellectus, which is our intuitive, imaginative reason which we grasp in an instant. Ratio is teleological - purpose driven - we ask questions and we get answers for some agenda we have (such as finding out the origins of a disease, and then finding a cure) The ratio of God is revealed by the underlying fundamental principles by which God has set up the world in the eternal law The world has deep structures of ratio which are revealed by scientific enquiry and also, structures of morality revealed by natural law.

Imagine I am looking at a rose.

First, I recognise it as "rose," and not as "peanut" or "shoe."
That doesn't take any effort on my part; I abstract the form of rose in an immediate intuition.

But then I can know the rose as a living rose. That is, I can let it act on me, receiving its shape and scent and colour in a timeless moment of contemplation. I am passive before it, receiving it "into me" as a "gift" worthy of praise, thanksgiving or imitation. That is to know it by intellectus.

But I can also act on the rose; I can analyse it. I count the number of leaves and thorns; describe the shape and colour. (I pull off the petals, one by one, and let them fall into a pile.) I can determine the number of petals. I can classify this rose as Damask or Noisette or Hybrid tea or Polyantha. I can breed new roses by removing all the petals and stamens of this rose and introducing the pollen of another rose. I can use rose hips to make a tea high in vitamin C. This is to know it by ratio.

Exercise 6.3: Explain how God's ratio is reflected in human ratio.

Teleological Map of Natural Law

"What is the good at which everyone aims?", asks Aristotle in Nichomachean Ethics. His reply: eudaimonia, the ultimate good of a flourishing and fulfilled life, fully lived.

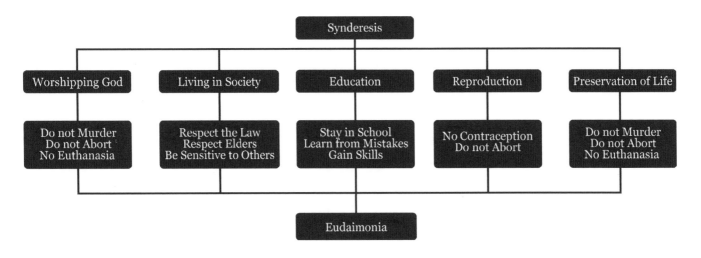

Exercise 6.4: One of the applications boxes (the secondary precepts below the primary precepts), is wrong. Correct this box for the correct secondary precepts.

Synderesis is the Starting Point

Synderesis is the intuitive knowledge of first principles (the primary precepts) and the desire, because we are made in the image of God, to pursue good ends (goals, telos = end). Aquinas calls this the 'first principle' of the natural law. It is the starting-point because we are all endowed by creation with this inbuilt knowledge of good and evil, and so it explains natural law theory's claim to be **universal**, applicable to both believer and non-believer.

The first principle of practical reason is one founded on the notion of good, that "good is that which all things seek after." Hence this is the first precept of law, that "good is to be done, and evil is to be avoided." All other precepts of the natural law are based upon this. (ST I-II Q94)

As the Roman Catholic encyclical Veritatis Splendor, 1995, expresses it:

"God cares for man not "from without", through the laws of physical nature, but "from within", through reason, which, by its natural knowledge of God's eternal law, is consequently able to show man the right direction to take in his free actions. In this way God calls man to participate in his own providence, since he desires to guide the world – not only the world of nature but also the world of human persons – through man himself, through man's reasonable and responsible care. The natural law is written and engraved in the heart of each and every man, since it is none other than human reason itself which commands us to do good and counsels us not to sin. It follows that the natural law is itself the eternal law, implanted in beings endowed with reason, and inclining them towards their right action and end; it is none other than the eternal reason of the Creator and Ruler of the universe". (Veritatis Splendor, 1995)

Primary Precepts

Aquinas argues for certain precepts of the natural law.

In man there is first of all an inclination to good in accordance with the nature which he has in common with all substances: inasmuch as every substance seeks the preservation of its own being, according to its nature: and by reason of this inclination, whatever is a means of preserving human life belongs to the natural law. Secondly, there is in man an inclination to things that pertain to him more specially, according to that nature which he has in common with other animals: and in virtue of this inclination, those things are said to belong to the natural law, "which nature has taught to all animals", such as sexual intercourse, education of offspring and so forth. Thirdly, there is in man an inclination to good, according to the nature of his reason, which nature is proper to him: thus man has a natural inclination to know the truth about God, and to live in society. (Aquinas, ST I-II Q94)

Exercise 6.5: Aquinas describes three levels of natural law which we share with substances, then with animals and then levels unique to human beings. Draw a table with three parts and explain each level of the natural law.

Acronym POWER

Exercise 6.6: These precepts spell the word (acronym) **POWER**. Draw up a table with three columns, one for the letter of the acronym, one for the primary precept and one for the secondary precepts. Remember:

Primary Precepts - absolute, general principles

Secondary precepts – specific rules and applications. Aquinas calls secondary precepts 'approximate conclusions of human reason' and these are **never absolute because they can change as we reflect and reason about consequences**.

Letter	Primary Precept	Secondary Precept
P		
O		
W		
E		
R		

The ultimate end is Eudaimonia – Aquinas talks about **felicitas** (happiness) in this life and **beatitudo** (blessedness or bliss) in heaven. We are empowered by God (the gift of **synderesis** for everyone, plus the Holy Spirit for Christians) to pursue moral ends which are in our best interest.

If you want a flourishing life you must orientate yourself to good, rational ends. These ends are the eternal law of the Designer (God).

Natural Law & Veritatis Splendor (1995)

Precisely because of this "truth" the natural law involves universality. Inasmuch as it is inscribed in the rational nature of the person, it makes itself felt to all beings endowed with reason and living in history. In order to perfect himself in his specific order, the person must do good and avoid evil, be concerned for the transmission and preservation of life, refine and develop the riches of the material world, cultivate social life, seek truth, practise good and contemplate beauty. (VS 51)

Consequently the moral life has an essential "teleological" character, since it consists in the deliberate ordering of human acts to God, the supreme good and ultimate end (telos) of man. (VS 73)

Exercise 6.7: There is no reference here to the primary precept, worship of God – but it is replaced by 'contemplate beauty'. What is the link between the two ideas?

Human Reason is Crucial

- It recognises the orientation to the good given by synderesis

- It determines **secondary precepts** (applications of general goods – primary precepts)

- It shows us what to do when two 'goods' conflict

Motive is Important

"It often happens that man acts with a good intention, but without spiritual gain, because he lacks a good will. Let us say that someone robs in order to feed the poor: in this case, even though the intention is good, the uprightness of the will is lacking. Consequently, no evil done with a good intention can be excused. 'There are those who say: And why not do evil that good may come? Their condemnation is just' (Rom 3:8)". (Aquinas, VS 78)

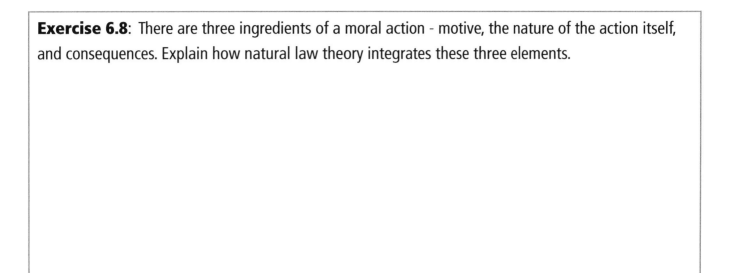

Exercise 6.8: There are three ingredients of a moral action - motive, the nature of the action itself, and consequences. Explain how natural law theory integrates these three elements.

When Two Goods Conflict

Aquinas introduces the **Principle of Double Effect**. If the intention (motive) is good, then the secondary effect can be ignored even if it is 'evil'.

A euthanasia example: a doctor visits a dying patient who is in a lot of pain. She tells the patient if she increases the morphine dose, the patient will die. The patient agrees.

Intention: to reduce suffering and pain. (Preservation of a dignified life)

Primary effect: pain is reduced.

Secondary effect: the patient dies. (Life is not preserved).

It is impossible both to reduce pain and preserve life. Double effect allows us to choose the right (arguably the most merciful) action.

Problem of Hierarchies in Natural Law

Up until 1649, we believed In the UK in the divine right of Kings. Then we executed Charles I for sedition (stirring up war against Parliament). Kings were top of a pyramid with peasants at the bottom.

In 1862 Andrew Stevens stood up in the Confederate Parliament and said this:

"I recollect once of having heard a gentleman from one of the northern States, of great power and ability, announce in the House of Representatives, with imposing effect, that we of the South would be compelled, ultimately, to yield upon this subject of slavery, that it was as impossible to war successfully against a principle in politics, as it was in physics or mechanics. That the principle would ultimately prevail. That we, in maintaining slavery as it exists with us, were warring against a principle, a principle founded in nature, the principle of the equality of men. The reply I made to him was, that upon his own grounds, we should, ultimately, succeed, and that he and his associates, in this crusade against our institutions, would ultimately fail. The truth announced, that it was as impossible to war successfully against a principle in politics as it was in physics and mechanics, I admitted; but told him that it was he, and those acting with him, who were warring against a principle. They were attempting to make things equal which the Creator had made unequal." (Andrew Stevens)

There is a **cornerstone principle**, said Stevens, that God made people unequal. Aristotle agreed: slaves and women were inferior, he thought. It was exactly this kind of argument that enraged the utilitarians like Mill, who espousing Bentham's equality principle, campaigned tirelessly against slavery. History, incidentally, is an excellent source of ethics case studies.

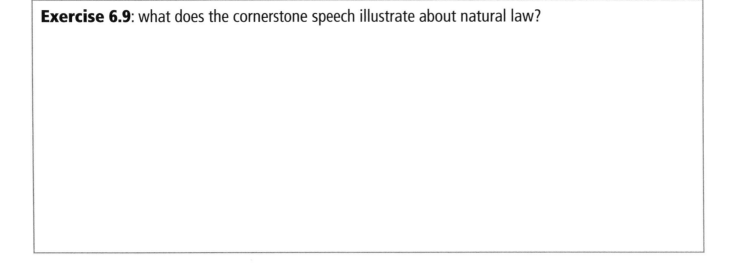

Exercise 6.9: what does the cornerstone speech illustrate about natural law?

Problem of Selfish Egoism

In Christianity there is a division between those who argue we are fundamentally **good,** because made in God's image, and those who say we are fundamentally **evil**, because infected by sin by the Fall of humankind (Christian Thought – Augustine).

Paul seems to argue **both** for inbuilt natural law and for human sinfulness.

"The Gentiles have the law written on their hearts". (Romans 2:14)

"I do not do what I want. The thing I hate is what I do". (Romans 7)

Exercise 6.10: Write a viewpoint on this fundamental point – 'original sin contradicts synderesis'. Do you agree?

Thought Point: In the Christian Thought paper (H573/3) we study Augustine and his views on the Fall in Genesis 3. Augustine believed sin was transmitted by male semen as a result of Adam and Eve's disobedience. Evangelical christians see humankind as fundamentally good, and Catholic Christians see humankind made int he image of God, endowed with synderesis and so fundamentally good.

Our human nature is orientated by natural law towards good ends, irrespective of whether we believe in God or not.

Essay-writing Skill

Exercise 6.11: Try a concluding paragraph on this question. Begin it by 'in conclusion….'

'The natural law is the participation in the eternal law by rational creatures'. (Aquinas, Summa Theologica I-II 91.2) Discuss

---

Example: "Natural law is the best approach to the ethical issues posed by euthanasia".

Answer: In conclusion, natural law is indeed the best approach to issues surrounding euthanasia, and superior to utilitarian ethics, for three reasons. First, it offers a flexibility due to the principle of double effect, whilst still recognising that when two goods conflict (pain prevention versus preservation of life) we cannot avoid making a choice. Secondly, unlike utilitarianism which makes no mention of motive, natural law retains an emphasis on the integrity of the moral character by emphasising right motive. Thirdly, natural law shares an element of consequentialism because, by exercising our right reason, given by God, we weigh consequences to build the flourishing life.

Deontological Ethics - Kant

Kant (1724-1804) argues that we build the moral ocean of goodness (the **summum bonum** or greatest good), drop by drop, by acting as **autonomous** rational beings in obedience to the **categorical imperative**.

We do this by concentrating on our **motive** – building the **'good will'** out of reverence for the moral law, which he says 'fills me with wonder'. This is very different from utilitarian ethics which emphasises measurable consequences, and **feelings** of pleasure and of sympathy.

Kant takes the Enlightenment Motto sapere aude (dare to reason) and applies it by an **a priori** method (before experience) to derive abstract categoricals which are then applied to real world situations. The morality of the act is divorced from the real-world situation and has **nothing** to do with consequences.

Deontological and Absolute

Robert Arrington calls Kantian ethics 'the stern-hearted ethics of duty". Is he right? Certainly Kant shifts the focus from consequences, to the idea of a duty to do the right thing irrespective of what it costs us.

Kantian ethics is absolute in all three meanings of the word **'absolute'**.

- **Universal** – based on a priori rationality which all humans share, to construct the moral law themselves by an imaginative process of universalising our action.

- **Non-consequentialist** – you can't have a categorical which looks at each situation individually, so Kantian ethics pays no attention at all to results.

- **Objective** – the moral law is an objective fact we access by reason.

Structure of Thought

```
                        ┌──────────────┐
                        │     Kant     │
                        └──────┬───────┘
                               │
                        ┌──────┴───────┐
                        │   Autonomy   │
                        └──────┬───────┘
                               │
                        ┌──────┴───────┐
                        │   a priori   │
                        └──────┬───────┘
                               │
                        ┌──────┴───────┐
                        │ Categoricals │
                        └──┬────┬────┬──┘
              ┌────────────┘    │    └────────────┐
  ┌───────────┴────────┐  ┌─────┴──────┐  ┌───────┴──────┐
  │ Formula of Autonomy│  │Formula of  │  │Formula of Law│
  └────────────────────┘  │   Ends     │  └──────────────┘
                          └─────┬──────┘
                        ┌───────┴──────┐
                        │Summum Bonum  │
                        └──────────────┘
```

Based on Motive and the 'Good Will'

Reason's true task is not the fulfilment of the needs of man, argues Kant. For such tasks, instinct is perfectly capable (Kant, Metaphysics, 62-70). Its place, rather, is the fulfilment of the good will.

Kant felt reason is "Given to us as a practical faculty, i.e. one which is meant to have an influence on the good will" (Kant 62 -67). But if reason exists and is a tool for all rational beings, what is the good will for which it is to be used?

The good will, according to Kant, is the only thing that is good in and of itself. Regardless of ends, disentangled from subjective wants and desires, the good will is its own end.

It is absolute and Kant argues

"to be esteemed incomparably higher than anything which could be brought about by it in favour of any inclination or even of the sum of total inclinations".

Or, more poetically,

"It would sparkle like a jewel in its own right, as something that has full worth in itself ".

Furthermore, what can best be understood as achieving the good will? Kant finds the closest human construct to emulating the carrying out of the good will is **duty**. For example, the man who tells his wife he cheated on her because it is his duty to treat other rational beings with honesty and respect is acting out of the good will.

Action alone out of duty, an obeying of the good will, is what constitutes moral actions. As Kant succinctly puts it,

"Thus the first proposition of morality is that to have moral worth an action must be done from duty" .

Exercise 7.1: what does Kant mean by 'the only good thing is the good will?'

Categorical, not Hypothetical

Hypotheticals have an 'if' in them. "If you are faced with a crazy knifeman at the door, wanting to know where your friend is hiding, you ought to lie".

Utilitarian ethics is based on hypotheticals. "If it would increase the general happiness, you should lock up terror suspects without trial, like in Guantanamo Bay".

Situation ethics is based on hypotheticals. "If love demands it, then lie".

In contrast, Kant argues: "you cannot universalise lying as it destroys the idea of truth. So never lie".

The statement 'never lie' is a maxim which is categorical (no ifs, no buts) and hence absolute.

Exercise 7.2: write your own hypothetical with the word **duty** in it, focusing on a situation involving Business Ethics.

Three Versions of the Categorical Imperative

Formula of Law: "so act that the maxim of your action can be willed as a universal law". (G4:402)

Formula of Ends: "never treat people as **simply** a means to an end, but always, **also**, as an end in themselves". What does this mean in terms of respecting others?

Formula of the Kingdom of Ends: 'Act as if through your maxims you were a law-making member of a kingdom of ends.' Is this just a combination of the first two formulations?

Kant is not telling us to ignore differences, to pretend that we are blind to them on mindless egalitarian grounds. However, a distinct way in which we respect persons, referred to as "recognition respect" by Stephen Darwall (1977), better captures Kant's position: I may respect you because you are a student, a Dean, a doctor or a mother. In such cases of respecting you because of who or what you are, I am giving the proper regard to a certain fact about you, your being a Dean for instance. This sort of respect, unlike appraisal respect, is not a matter of degree based on your having measured up to some standard of assessment. Respect for the humanity in persons is more like Darwall's recognition respect. We are to respect human beings simply because they are persons and this requires a certain sort of regard. We are not called on to respect them insofar as they have met some standard of evaluation appropriate to persons. And, crucially for Kant, persons cannot lose their humanity by their misdeeds – even the most vicious persons, Kant thought, deserve basic respect as persons with humanity. (Stanford Encyclopaedia)

Exercise 7.3: in your own words explain what it means to treat someone as 'an end in themselves". As a clue, Professor Norman describes this as 'universalising your shared humanity' or 'treating the other person as if you were that person yourself'. Watch this three minute summary: https://www.youtube.com/watch?v=xwOCmJevigw

The Three Postulates

Kant puts forward three **postulates** (things he makes no attempt to prove, but simply postulates). These are:

1. **Autonomy** – we make the moral law for ourselves using our free reason (autonomous, in Greek, self-law).

2. **God**

3. **Immortality**

Exercise 7.4: Research and explain why Kant needs the postulates (assumptions) of God and immortality. After all, isn't Kantian ethics supremely the ethics of reason?

Thought Points

1. John Hick is inspired by Kant's idea of the unaccessible **noumenal** realm, where God dwells. (see Hick's Universal Pluralism in Christian Thought H573/3).

2. Plato's ideal **Forms** echo Kant's inaccessible noumena (Philosophy of Religion H573/1).

3. Jesus' maxim 'do to others as you would have them do to you' (The Golden Rule Matthew 7.12) echoes Kantian universalisability. If you research the Golden Rule website, you will find versions of this maxim in all major world religions.

Deontological or Teleological?

The received view is that Kant's moral philosophy is a deontological normative theory at least to this extent: it denies that right and wrong are in some way or other functions of goodness or badness. It denies, in other words, the central claim of teleological moral views. For instance, act consequentialism is one sort of teleological theory. It asserts that the right action is that action of all the alternatives available to the agent that has the best overall outcome. Here, the goodness of the outcome determines the rightness of an action. Another sort of teleological theory might focus instead on character traits. "Virtue ethics" asserts that a right action in any given circumstance is that action a virtuous person does or would perform in those circumstances. In this case, it is the goodness of the character of the person who does or would perform it that determines the rightness of an action. In both cases, as it were, the source or ground of rightness is goodness. And Kant's own views have typically been classified as deontological precisely because they have seemed to reverse this priority and deny just what such theories assert. Rightness, on the standard reading of Kant, is not grounded in the value of outcomes or character, but on the nature of the act itself, and on motive. (Stanford Encyclopaedia)

Evaluating Kant

Kantian ethics differs from utilitarian ethics both in its scope and in the precision with which it guides action. Every action, whether of a person or of an agency, can be assessed by utilitarian methods, provided only that information is available about all the consequences of the act. The theory has unlimited scope, but owing to lack of data, often lacks precision. Kantian ethics has a more restricted scope. Since it assesses actions by looking at the maxims of agents, it can only assess intentional acts. This means that it is most at home in assessing individuals' acts; but it can be extended to assess acts of agencies that (like corporations and governments and student unions) have decision-making procedures. It can do nothing to assess patterns of action that reflect no intention or policy, hence it cannot assess the acts of groups lacking decision-making procedures, such as the student movement, the women's movement, or the consumer movement.

It may seem a great limitation of Kantian ethics that it concentrates on intentions to the neglect of results. It might seem that all conscientious Kantians have to do is to make sure that they never intend to use others as mere means, and that they sometimes intend to foster other's ends. And, as we all know, good intentions sometimes lead to bad results and correspondingly, bad intentions sometimes do no harm, or even produce good. If Hardin is right, the good intentions of those who feed the starving lead to dreadful results in the long run. If some traditional arguments in favor of capitalism are right, the greed and selfishness of the profit motive have produced unparalleled prosperity for many.

But such discrepancies between intentions and results are the exception and not the rule. For we cannot just claim that our intentions are good and do what we will. Our intentions reflect what we expect the immediate results of our action to be. Nobody credits the "intentions" of a couple who practise neither celibacy nor contraception but still insist "we never meant to have (more) children." Conception is likely (and known to be likely) in such cases. Where people's expressed intentions ignore the normal and predictable results of what they do, we infer that (if they are not amazingly ignorant) their words do not express their true intentions. The Formula of the End in Itself applies to the intentions on which one acts--not to some prettified version that one may avow. Provided this intention--the agent's real intention--uses no other as mere means, he or she does nothing unjust. If some of his or her intentions foster others' ends, then he or she is sometimes beneficent. It is therefore possible for people to test their proposals by Kantian arguments even when they lack the comprehensive causal knowledge that utilitarianism requires. Conscientious Kantians can work out whether they will be doing wrong by some act even though they know that their foresight is limited and that they may cause some harm or fail to cause some benefit. But they will not cause harms that they can foresee without this being reflected in their intentions. (source: Onara O'Neill)

Exercise 7.5: List three evaluative points you might use from Onara O'Neill's evaluation of Kant.

Essay-writing Skills

Exercise 7.6: Try an eight paragraph structure.

"Kantian ethics is the best approach to issues surrounding business ethics". Discuss

Paragraph 1 Thesis statement (include the issues surrounding business ethics)

Paragraph 2 Development

Paragraph 3 Counter-point

Paragraph 4 Development

Paragraph 5 Counter-point

Paragraph 6 Development

Paragraph 7 Counter-point

Paragraph 8 Conclusion

Example: 'Utilitarian approaches to business ethics exploit vulnerable workers'. Discuss

Thesis

Business ethics concerns how we treat people, whether profit is the best motive, and how much we value the environment. Utilitarianism is not the best approach because it is too pragmatic.

Development

Mill's utilitarianism different to Bentham's as Mill stresses social context and justice rather than just pleasure.

Counter-point

A case study such as Ford Pinto indicates how duty may be stronger eg duty to put customers' interests above profit

Development

May depend which form of utilitarianism we are talking about as Mill stresses sympathy for everyone and Bentham - we should give everyone equal weight which Pinto case didn't do

Counter-point

Kantian ethics doesn't allow su to look at consequences at all, but universal maxims like 'always tell the truth'. Apply to Pinto case.

Development

Problem – sometimes two moral goods conflict eg employment of workers needs profit, but profit may involve dumping toxic waste or reducing safety criteria (as in Pinto)

Counter-point

Utilitarianism better than Kantian ethics in handling complexity and moral dilemmas – as long as equal consideration of all stakeholder interests is kept paramount

Conclusion

Utilitarianism is on balance weaker than Kantian duties in ensuring non-pragmatic decisions which take all interests into account. Ford Pinto shows we can't calculate consequences accurately.

Euthanasia (Natural Law and Situation Ethics)

Issues

- Which is more important morally - Sanctity – sacredness, or Quality of Life (and the right to choose)?

- Is "thou shalt not kill' **absolute** (think of war, death penalty, punishments for various sins in Leviticus)?

Christian churches allow forms of non-intervention eg "since resuscitation techniques go beyond the ordinary means to which one is bound, it cannot be held that there is an obligation to use them or, consequently, that one is bound to give the doctor permission to use them." Pope Pius

- Passive/active euthanasia - is there a moral difference between an **act** (actively administering a drug to kill someone) and an **omission** (failing to act to prolong a life, or withdrawing treatment that might sustain life)?

- Voluntary/non-voluntary euthanasia - how morally important is a patient's consent?

"The sanctity of life position has always maintained that there are instances where letting a person die, or even killing another human being, is ethically right". (John Quilter Babies Doe, page 3)

Situation Ethics and Euthanasia

Joseph Fletcher was a lifelong supporter of euthanasia.

- **Quality of Life** must be considered (a consequentialist argument - what are the prospects of good quality of life?)

- The person's interests must come first (**personalism**)

- **Love** demands we don't allow someone to die a 'slow and ugly death' (Fletcher)

- Love comes before law and moral rules (no **absolutes**)

- The **end** justifies the means – even in non-voluntary euthanasia (Schindler's List example - the doctors administer drugs to kill patients in the ghetto just as Nazi machine guns can be heard outside in the street)

Problems with Situation Ethics

- Who decides?

- How do we value **'useless life'**? What about a person in a Persistent Vegetative State (PSV), such as Tony Bland (died 1993, the) Hillsborough football stadium disaster victim (1989).

- Fletcher underplays the **principle of consent** – "The day will come when people will be able to carry a card, notarised and legally executed, which explains that they do not want to 'be kept alive beyond the humane point" (Fletcher)

- Paul Ramsey 'there is a categorical imperative: 'never abandon care'. (1970:134)

Exercise 8.1: Evaluate the situationist approach to euthanasia as applied to the case of Tony Bland.

Starmer Guidelines (2010)

- How likely is a prosecution for assisting suicide?

- Financial interest

- Undue pressure

- Consent

- Of the 250 Dignitas suicides (eg Daniel James) few have been investigated

"The policy is now more focused on the motivation of the suspect rather than the characteristics of the victim." Keir Starmer

Exercise 8.2: What were the Starmer guidelines? What moral and legal issues were they seeking to clarify?

Oregon Rules (1997)

The state of Oregon, USA passed rules for assisted dying into law in 1997. Here are some examples.

- You must self-medicate

- Over 18

- Consent of two doctors (15 days gap)

- Terminally ill

- Doctor in attendance

- Must be given palliative care option

995 people have died in ten years since the state of Oregon legalised assisted dying, (an average of two per week)

Slippery Slope Arguments

Slippery slope arguments state that, if the law banning euthanasia is changed, then society will slide into a very dangerous and undesirable place.

- An empirical issue (to do with outcomes)

- Based on probabilities - what is the most likely result?

- Legal checks to stop the slide

- Numbers in Oregon state (which has assisted dying) are small (about 100 people a year)

Exercise 8.3 Write a paragraph evaluating this statement: 'if euthanasia is legalised, it will initiate a slippery slope".

Integrity Problem

- Bernard Williams argues there are some things we just cannot do, because they violate our own integrity. Will legalising euthanasia be against the integrity of doctors who have taken the Hippocratic Oath always to do their best to preserve life?

- Bruce Vortuga argues euthanasia 'dehumanises us all'. "The quantification Fletcher advocates for determining the quality of life and those persons qualified to retain it, in a very real sense, dehumanise us all". Bruce Vortuga

- Utilitarian argument against euthanasia – **society** is generally less happy if we know we have certain choices such as the ability to be helped to die.

A Doctor's View

"There is a myth that doctors are there to prolong life; they are not. Their prime purpose is to relieve suffering; if life is prolonged as a result, well and good. The medical profession has got these ideals confused." Dr Hooper

---

Exercise 8.4: Research the Hippocratic Oath, Does euthanasia violate the oath?

Autonomy and Consent

- Act-based theories (such as situation ethics) emphasise autonomy

- How free (autonomous) are we?

- Depression

- Financial loss

- Increase in life expectancy/elderly population

- Family tensions

Sanctity of Life and Natural Law Precepts

Sanctity of life arguments (apart from Kantian ones) maintain it is sometimes right to kill another human being (or let them die). The issue is: what are those conditions? Natural Law allows for situations of **Double Effect**. Here is the papal encyclical, Veritatis Splendor (1995), on his subject.

79. One must therefore reject the thesis, characteristic of teleological and proportionalist theories, which holds that it is impossible to qualify as morally evil according to its species — its "object" — the deliberate choice of certain kinds of behaviour or specific acts, apart from a consideration of the intention for which the choice is made or the totality of the foreseeable consequences of that act for all persons concerned.

The primary and decisive element for moral judgment is the object of the human act, which establishes whether it is capable of being ordered to the good and to the ultimate end, which is God. This capability is grasped by reason in the very being of man, considered in his integral truth, and therefore in his natural inclinations, his motivations and his goals, which always have a spiritual dimension as well. It is precisely these which are the contents of the natural law and hence that ordered complex of "personal goods" which serve the "good of the person": the good which is the person himself and his perfection. These are the goods safeguarded by the commandments, which, according to Saint Thomas, contain the whole natural law.

The Second Vatican Council itself, in discussing the respect due to the human person, gives a number of examples of such acts: "Whatever is hostile to life itself, such as any kind of homicide, genocide, abortion, euthanasia and voluntary suicide; whatever violates the integrity of the human person, such as mutilation, physical and mental torture and attempts to coerce the spirit; whatever is offensive to human dignity, such as subhuman living conditions, arbitrary imprisonment, deportation, slavery, prostitution and trafficking in women and children; degrading conditions of work which treat labourers as mere instruments of profit, and not as free responsible persons: all these and the like are a disgrace, and so long as they infect human civilization they contaminate those who inflict them more than those who suffer injustice, and they are a negation of the honour due to the Creator". Veritatis Splendor 1995

Exercise 8.5: in the above extract from Veritatis Splendor, explain the statements below:

1. "The primary and decisive element for moral judgment is **the object of the human act,** which establishes whether it is capable of being ordered to the good and to the ultimate end, which is God". (Object here means telos or purpose).

2. "**Whatever is hostile to life itself, such as any kind of homicide, genocide, abortion, euthanasia and voluntary suicide**; whatever violates the integrity of the human person, all these and the like are a disgrace, and so long as they infect human civilization they contaminate those who inflict them more than those who suffer injustice, and they are a negation of the honour due to the Creator".

Religious Origins of the Sanctity of Life

1. We are all made in God's image 'male and female he created them', and we are all declared good – "and God saw that it was good'. Genesis 1:27

2. The Bible mixes law and wisdom. Wisdom warns and counsels us to be careful. "There is a time to mourn, and a time to die". Ecclesiastes 3:2

3. Covenantal fidelity implies we are faithful to a higher value no matter what the consequences. Paul Ramsey argues for this in Ethics at the Edge of Life.

4. St Augustine argues that 'thou shalt not kill' applies to suicide (active euthanasia).

5. Aquinas argues suicide is a **mortal sin** which injures the community and violates the primary precept of preservation of life. "For it belongs to God alone to pronounce sentence of death and life, according to Dt. 32:39, "I will kill and I will make to live.""

Exercise 8.6: Sanctity of Human Life is an absolute. Is it? Explain your reasons.

Secular Arguments for Sanctity of Life

Deontologists such as Kantian or natural law philosophers tend to argue for an absolute right to life, although they derive this right from different sources. A Kantian derives it from **the categorical imperative**, whereas a natural law ethicist (or the Roman Catholic Church) would derive the right from the **primary precept** of the preservation of life.

Kantian sanctity of life implies we "do not just treat people as a means to an end but also as ends in themselves" and so with absolute dignity and respect for their autonomy. Don't use yourself as a means to an end by committing suicide.

Natural law – although the right to life is absolute, it is sometimes impossible to avoid the evil of killing someone. Aquinas' example is self-defence. The right to life is reflected in the absolute primary principle Preserve Life – but when applying this a secondary percept we can find two moral goods are in conflict and it is impossible to 'have both'. So we have to act, but do not intend the second evil effect.

Quality of Life

The First New Commandment: Recognise that the worth of human life varies". Peter Singer

It may be possible, now, to eliminate pain. In almost all cases, it may even be possible to do it in a

way that leaves patients in possession of their rational faculties and free from vomiting, nausea, or other distressing side-effects. Unfortunately only a minority of dying patients now receive this kind of care. Nor is physical pain the only problem. There can also be other distressing conditions, like bones so fragile they fracture at sudden movements, uncontrollable nausea and vomiting, slow starvation due to a cancerous growth, inability to control one's bowels or bladder, difficulty in breathing, and so on. (Peter Singer)

Exercise 8.7: summarise Peter Singer's utilitarian viewpoint. He lists some conditions which define a good quality of life: the categories "being", "belonging", and "becoming"; respectively who I am, howl am not connected to my environment, and whether I am able to achieve my personal goals, hopes, and aspirations.

Acts and Omissions

The British Medical Association Working Party are commendably clear in recognising the law's deep-seated adherence to intent rather than consequences alone as an important reference point in the moral assessment of any action. A decision to withdraw treatment which has become a burden and is no longer of continuing benefit to a patient has a different intent to one which involves ending the life of a person. We accept drug treatment which may involve a risk to the patient's life if the sole intention is to relieve illness, pain, distress or suffering. Accepting the central importance of intention to the characterisation and, therefore, the evaluation of chosen actions, the Working Party reject the view that it is only outcomes or consequences which should count in the moral evaluation of actions. On this latter, characteristically utilitarian view there is no significant moral distinction between hastening death as a foreseeable consequence of the administration of drugs aimed at controlling pain, and bringing about death as a result of administering a lethal dose of drugs aimed precisely at bringing about death. BMA Working Party

James Rachels argues there is no difference between an **act (actively assisting someone)** and an **omission (failure to act to continue treatment)** if the intention is the same. He uses an analogy of Smith, Jones and the bath.

Smith and Jones both stand to inherit quite a bit of money upon the death of their young nephew, so both want that child dead. Smith sneaks into the bathroom one night when his nephew is taking a bath and drowns him, then arranges things to make it look like an accident. In the second case, Jones sneaks into the bathroom one night when his nephew is taking a bath, prepared to drown him, but then the boy slips, hits his head, and drowns all on his own. Jones is ready to push the child's head back down under the water, but he doesn't have to. The only difference between the two cases is that one involves killing and the other involves letting die, but what Jones did is just as morally bad as what Smith did, so there's no moral difference between them. There's no moral difference between killing and letting die. (James Rachels)

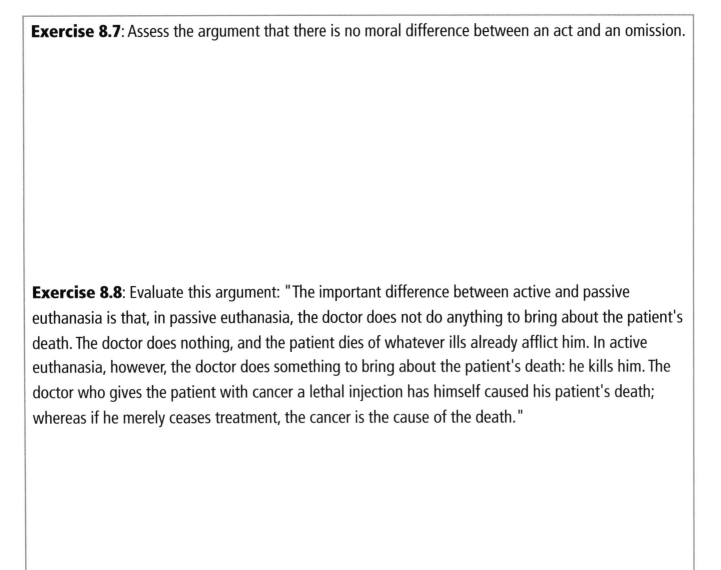

Exercise 8.7: Assess the argument that there is no moral difference between an act and an omission.

Exercise 8.8: Evaluate this argument: "The important difference between active and passive euthanasia is that, in passive euthanasia, the doctor does not do anything to bring about the patient's death. The doctor does nothing, and the patient dies of whatever ills already afflict him. In active euthanasia, however, the doctor does something to bring about the patient's death: he kills him. The doctor who gives the patient with cancer a lethal injection has himself caused his patient's death; whereas if he merely ceases treatment, the cancer is the cause of the death."

Exercise 8.9: Consider this example (different because here the intention is good, whereas with Rachels' example, it's bad).

I drive my boat to the lake one Saturday, and I see one person clinging to a rock on one side of the lake, and five people clinging to a rock on the other side of the lake. I want to save some folks from death, and everyone will drown if I don't do something, but I can only save either the one or the five. I motor over to the five and save them, letting the one die. In the second case, I'm driving my boat to the lake one Saturday, and I see five people offshore, clinging to a rock, clearly about to drown. I can – and want to – save them, but only by driving over one person who's unconscious on the loading dock. I nevertheless drive over him, killing him, but I manage to save the five in so doing. Now it seems there's a moral difference between a killing and letting die case, and that – the killing case – is morally worse than – the letting die case.

Is there a moral difference between the two cases? What is it?

Principle of Double Effect

The Roman Catholic Church allows for Double Effect (first argued by Aquinas)

2278: Discontinuing medical procedures that are burdensome, dangerous, extraordinary, or disproportionate to the expected outcome can be legitimate; it is the refusal of "over-zealous" treatment. Here one does not will to cause death; one's inability to impede it is merely accepted. The decisions should be made by the patient if he is competent and able or, if not, by those legally entitled to act for the patient, whose reasonable will and legitimate interests must always be respected.

2279: Even if death is thought imminent, the ordinary care owed to a sick person cannot be legitimately interrupted. The use of painkillers to alleviate the sufferings of the dying, even at the risk of shortening their days, can be morally in conformity with human dignity if death is not willed as either an end or a means, but only foreseen and tolerated as inevitable. Palliative care is a special form of disinterested charity. As such it should be encouraged. Catholic Catechism

Exercise 8.10: How might the argument in the Catechism be applied to someone in a Persistent Vegetative State (PSV). Does this mean the Catholic Church accepts the difference between an 'act' and an 'omission', such as not applying 'overzealous' treatment to someone who is dying?

Essay-writing

Exercise 8.11: Try writing opening paragraphs for the following two questions.

1. "There is no moral difference between active and passive euthanasia". Discuss

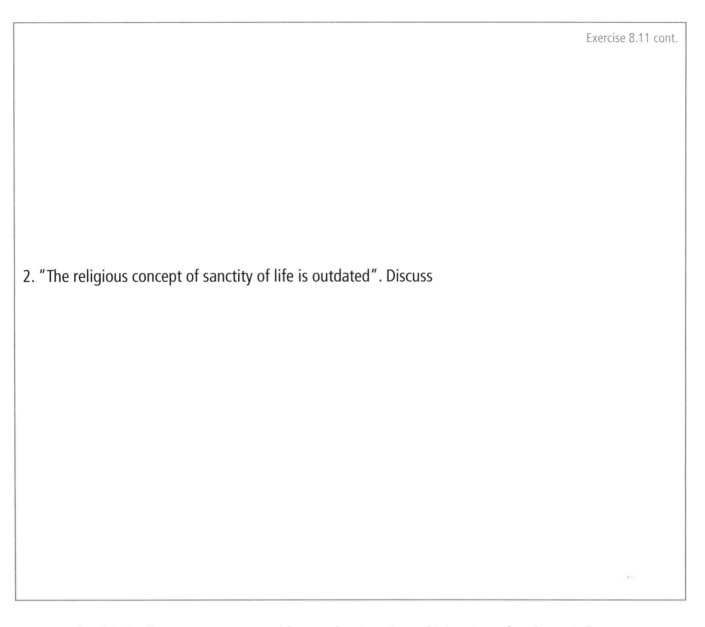

2. "The religious concept of sanctity of life is outdated". Discuss

Example: "Critically compare a natural law and a situation ethicist view of euthanasia".

Answer: A natural law view, such as Aquinas', argues that human beings are designed with rational purposes that include, amongst others, living in society and preservation of life. We share a common human nature which orientates us towards the good through the synderesis principle. This still admits of complexity, because natural law theorists allow for a principle of double effect to help us decide, for instance, what to do when a patient near death is suffering extreme pain. Generally the Catholic Church has issued an absolute prohibition on euthanasia as 'intrinsically evil'. Situationists disagree: following Fletcher they take a pragmatic case by case approach which views quality of life as more meaningful than sanctity of life. But does the allegation that natural law is inflexible on sanctity issues hold good? And does Situation ethics deny the social consequences of any change in euthanasia law, in generating a climate of possible fear and uncertainty amongst the elderly, irrespective of individual cases?

Business Ethics (Applied to Kant and Utilitarianism)

Key Issues

The specification requires us to apply Kantian ethics and Utilitarianism to issues surrounding business ethics.

Exercise 9.1: Research and try to work out what moral issues are involved in the following terms listed in the specification.

Globalisation

Whistle-blowing

Profit motive

Stakeholder Interests

Corporate Social Responsibility (& Stakeholder Theory)

"Corporate Responsibility is about ensuring that organisations manage their businesses to make a positive impact on society and the environment whilst maximising value for their shareholders."
Institute of Chartered Accountants in England & Wales

Is Milton Friedman Right?

Professor Milton Friedman argued in 1978 that businesses need to concentrate on making money and leave the moral framework to Government legislation. It is for society to agree 'the rules of the game'.

"There is one and only one social responsibility of business to use its resources and engage in activities designed to increase its profits so long as it stays in the rules of the game, which is to say, engages in open and free competition, without deception or fraud".

"A corporate executive … has direct responsibility to conduct business in accordance with shareholder desires, to make as much money as possible while conforming to the basic rules of the society, both those embodied in law and those embodied in ethical custom."

"There has been the claim that business should contribute to support charitable activities and especially to universities. Such giving by corporations is an inappropriate use of corporate funds in a free-enterprise society." Milton Friedman

---

Exercise 9.2: Evaluate Friedman's view in the light of the concept of **corporate social responsibility**. Is Friedman arguing for a form of social Darwinism – survival of the fittest corporation? Notice he is **not** arguing businesses should ignore morality.

```
[empty box]
```

Problem - Ethics or Economics?

To maximise the welfare (or happiness) of everyone may harm the long-term prospects of the business.

Solution – Argue for Utilitarian Gains for Ethical Behaviour

Is ethical business actually good marketing? Here are some possible benefits:

- Improved productivity (output per hour) of the workforce

- Improved community relations (and trade-off of community benefits in exchange for planning consent)

- Improved financial performance may result if…

- Improved image with consumers and hence marketability of products

- Improved share price – of shareholders are looking for ethical elements to a business

- Improved recruitment of top-level staff – eg graduates may be seeking ethical element

- Improved environmental protection

Exercise 9.3 Outline a utilitarian case for being ethical in business.

Kant's Approach

Does **globalisation** put good business ahead of good ethics, as companies seek the lowest tax, lowest wage, least regulated country?

Kant argues for a moral duty created by the categorical imperative – the motive of 'good will' is the key.

A Kantian approach to business is echoed by the Companies Act which talks about '**fiduciary duties**' or duties of care directors have towards all stakeholders.

Exercise 9.4: Define the categorical imperative (two versions)

Write an opening paragraph on this question: ''The only good thing is the good will'. Kant rules out a profit motive as the primary motive in business. Discuss

Three Case Studies On Business Ethics

Case Study 1: Trafigura and Toxic Waste 2006

- Profit (shareholders) in conflict with duty of care to Ivory Coast citizens

- Poisonous gas kills 17 people and affects hundreds (by-product of the petroleum waste from Trafigura tanker)

Case Study 2: Enron 2003

Enron had a whistle-blower (finance director Sherron Watkins, 2001)

She put forward her concerns a year before Enron collapsed, to chairman Ken Lay.

Should she have gone to the police?

Exercise 9.5: Consider whether whistleblowing in the Enron collapse might have saved the company from financial disaster. Is whistleblowing just too heroic and self-sacrificial to be morally realistic?

Case Study 3 Bernie Madhoff and Kant – a Ponzi Scheme

Bernie Madoff claimed that the **Ponzi scheme** (a scheme which uses revenue from new clients to finance exorbitant returns to existing clients) wasn't the original idea. He sought money from investors planning to make big money with complicated financial manoeuvres. He took a few losses early on and faced the possibility of everyone just taking their cash and going home. That's when he started channelling money from new investors to older ones, claiming the funds were the fruit of his excellent stock dealing (which was a lie). He always intended, Madoff says, to get the money back, score some huge successes, and they'd let him get on the straight and narrow again. It never happened. But that doesn't change the fact that Madoff thought it would. He was lying temporarily, and for the good of everyone in the long run.

Exercise 9.6: Why is lying always wrong, according to Kant?

Conclusions

1. **Consistency**. What Kant's categorical imperative shows is that lying cannot be universalised. The act of lying can't survive in a world where everyone's just making stuff up all the time. Since no one will be taking anyone else seriously, you may try to sell a false story but no one will be buying it.

2. **Dignity**. Where the first of the categorical imperative's expressions was a consistency principle (treat others the way you want to be treated), this is a dignity principle: treat others with respect and as holding value in themselves. You will act ethically, according to Kant, as long as you never accept the temptation to treat others as a way to get something else.

3. **Integrity**. This involves motive – if we make a mistake, if our motive is pure we can't be blamed for making an 'honest mistake'. If our motive is impure (for profit) we will very likely be blamed.

Remember Bernard Williams' integrity objection to utilitarian ethics? Kant scores over utilitarianism in all three areas – consistency (and trust is good for business), dignity (no-one is exploited) and integrity (we are true to our beliefs).

Further reading try this excellent website on Kant and Business Ethics, and the second one, on Business Ethics and Friedman

https://catalog.flatworldknowledge.com/bookhub/1695?e=brusseau-ch02_s03

https://lucidmanager.org/essays/milton-friedman/

Essay-writing

Exercise 9.7: Write an opening paragraph on these two questions.

1. "Kantian ethics is the best approach to issues surrounding business ethics." Discuss.

2. Critically compare the ethical approaches to business of Kantian ethics and Utilitarianism.

Meta-ethics

Meta-Ethics means 'beyond ethics'. It concerns the **meaning** of moral terms, not the **derivation** of moral norms (normative ethics).

Three Issues in Meta-ethics

1. What is the foundation of ethics? Is the foundation **naturalistic** (a natural feature of the world)?

2. What does the word 'good' mean? Does it have a unique meaning, different from, say, observing 'that's a good picture!'?

3. Is moral language meaningful? If so, in what sense? is the meaning just subjective (like 'that's a good picture')?

Three Terms & Three Applications

Naturalism: the belief that values can be defined in terms of some natural property in the world, and its application to **absolutism**

Intuitionism: the belief that basic moral truths are indefinable but self-evident, and its application to the term **'good'**

Emotivism: the belief that ethical terms evince approval or disapproval, and its application to **relativism**

Specification

Asks us to consider:

- Whether or not what is meant by the word 'good' is the defining question in the study of ethics

- Whether or not ethical terms such as good, bad, right and wrong:

78

- have an objective factual basis that makes them true or false in describing something

- reflect only what is in the mind of the person using such terms

- can be said to be meaningful or meaningless whether or not, from a common sense approach, people just know within themselves what is good, bad, right and wrong

Structure of Thought

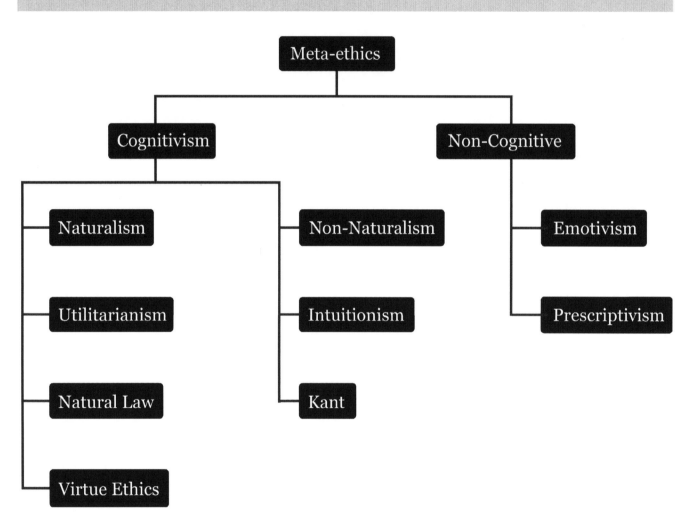

The Debate about Moral Facts

David Hume (1711-1776) and AJ Ayer (1910-1989) reject the idea that there is such a thing as a 'moral fact'. There are simply descriptions of what we see (for example 'there is a dead body'). The moral part is a judgement I make which I impose on this fact ("How terrible! A murder!).

Notice how naturalistic philosophies take different views about what this 'fact' might be.

Philosophy	Idea of Goodness	Moral fact
Natural law	**Eudaimonia** - a future state of personal and social flourishing	An internal and external **state** where the primary precepts are fulfilled and realised
Utilitarianism	**Pleasure** or Happiness	A **feeling** which we experience a posteriori which all human beings seek
Situation Ethics	**Agape** love	An **attitude** we live by which we embrace by faith which leads to **state** of well-being for everyone

Note:

1. Kant's theory is **non-naturalistic** – because it's based on an **a priori** imaginative process of reasoning called universalisation.

2. Intuitionism was hated by the utilitarians as a non-naturalistic philosophy. "Intuitionism is an instrument devised for consecrating deep-seated prejudices", said JS Mill.

Exercise 10.1: In the table above, how many of these 'facts' can be objectively verified? Are they nonetheless meaningful?

David Hume's Missing Premise Argument

In every system of morality, which I have hitherto met with, I have always remarked, that the author proceeds for some time in the ordinary way of reasoning, and establishes the being of a God, or makes observations concerning human affairs; when of a sudden I am surprised to find, that instead of the usual copulations of propositions, is, and is not, I meet with no proposition that is not connected with an ought, or an ought not. This change is imperceptible; but is, however, of the last consequence. For as this ought, or ought not, expresses some new relation or affirmation, 'tis necessary that it should be observed and explained; and at the same time that a reason should be given, for what seems altogether inconceivable, how this new relation can be a deduction from others, which are entirely different from it. But as authors do not commonly use this precaution, I shall presume to recommend it to the readers; and am persuaded, that this small attention would subvert all the vulgar systems of morality, and let us see, that the distinction of vice and virtue is not founded merely on the relations of objects, nor is perceived by reason. (David Hume, Treatise of Human Nature. p. 469-470).

Notice that Hume wants to rule 'offside' the 'vulgar systems of morality' and also 'the being of a God'. He is attacking the premise (stage of the argument) that is missing when we move from saying 'this is pleasurable' to 'this is morally good'. Although Hume implies it is 'inconceivable' how we can do this (and himself believes moral statements are based on feelings of sympathy and antipathy), his is really a challenge to naturalists to supply the **missing premise**.

Exercise 10.2: What is so 'good' about pleasure? Can we answer this question?

The Naturalistic Fallacy

You cannot move from an 'is' to an 'ought', argued GE Moore and to do so commits the **naturalistic fallacy** of applying a moral judgement to descriptive facts.

"It may be true that all things which are good are also something else, just as it is true that all things which are yellow produce a certain kind of vibration in the light. And it is a fact, that ethics aims at discovering what are those other properties belonging to all things which are good. But far too many philosophers have thought that when they named those other properties they were actually defining good; that these properties, in fact, were simply not "other," but absolutely and entirely the same with goodness. This view I propose to call the "naturalistic fallacy" and of it I shall now endeavour to dispose." (Principia Ethica § 10 ¶ 3)

You cannot add some extra property to pleasure that makes pleasure good –pleasure just is pleasure.

Goodness is "one of those innumerable objects of thought which are themselves incapable of definition, because they are the ultimate terms by reference to which whatever is capable of definition must be defined".

Intuitionists argue that goodness is a non-definable, non-reducible, non-naturalistic property of an action, which we grasp by intuition, like the colour yellow.

Problems with Moore's Intuitionist View

1. Goodness is a **complex** property like colour (not yellow). It isn't **simple** (one-dimensional) as Moore argues.

2. Most ethical theories do derive an ought from an is. The question is, do they do so validly?

3. Moreover, Moore's own theory is susceptible to the open question attack - "that may be your intuition, Mr Moore, but is it good?"

82

Defences of Naturalism

Utilitarians say goodness can be derived by **observation**. Just see what people are pursuing, and what they are avoiding, says Mill, and you will observe they maximise pleasure and minimise pain. An empirical test for goodness,

Natural Law theorists argue that goodness is implanted by God (**synderesis**) and also observable **a posteriori** in the goals people pursue. An experiential, empirical test.

Situation Ethics argues that goodness is accepted by **faith**, then proved by **experience**. The first step, **positivism**, seems to agree with Moore, as Fletcher argues we cannot prove intrinsic goodness for anything.

Open Question Attack

Used by Moore and Ayer.

It still makes sense to ask the further question of a natural property of goodness (such as utilitarian pleasure): 'it may be pleasurable, but is it good?'. It's an 'open question' whether pleasure is good or not (and indeed, some pleasures may be very bad).

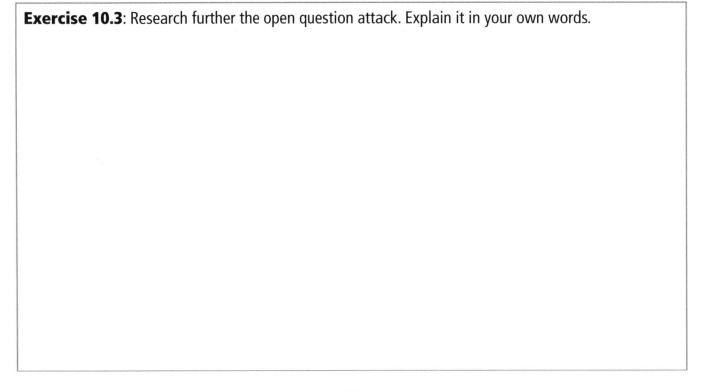

Exercise 10.3: Research further the open question attack. Explain it in your own words.

The Analytic/Synthetic Divide

The argument about the meaningfulness of language originates with David Hume. Statements about the real world are either analytic or synthetic, said Hume Moral language is neither, and hence empirically and analytically meaningless.

Example:

1. All bachelors are unmarried (analytic)

2. John Smith is a bachelor (synthetic)

3. "Is bachelor John Smith married?" (meaningless and stupid)

4. "Killing is wrong" (meaningless, but hold on, don't we seem to know what it means?)

Emotivism

AJ Ayer argued that statements about reality needed to be **verified** true or false according to sense experience. Ethical statements had no factual content as they could not be verified true or false.

Take, for example, the utilitarian proposition that things are good or bad according to the pleasure or pain produced.

So "goodness" here is a natural property of an action because it can be measured by consequences, (the "naturalistic fallacy" below).

"It is not self-contradictory to say some pleasant things are not good, or that some bad things are desired." (Ayer, 1971:139).

So, argues Ayer, if we can still ask the question "is it good?" after we have asked "is it pleasurable?", then goodness or badness must mean something else other than the pleasure or pain produced.

Ayer goes on to argue:

"The presence of an ethical symbol in a proposition adds nothing to its factual content. Thus if I say to someone, "you acted wrongly in stealing that money", I am not saying anything more than

if I had said simply "you stole that money". In adding that this action is wrong I am not making any further statement about it. I am simply evincing my moral disapproval of it. It is as if I said "you stole that money" in a peculiar tone of horror, or written it with the addition of some special exclamation marks." (Ayer, 1971:142)

So Ayer concludes that moral statements are primarily expressions of emotion, hence "emotivism", although he goes on to hint at something else as well:

"it is worth mentioning that ethical terms do not serve only to express feeling, but to arouse feeling, and so to stimulate action." (1971:143)

So if I find a dead body on the park and exclaim: "How terrible, it's murder!" there are actually no additional **moral** facts to point to in addition to the descriptive fact of the dead body. We have (my metaphor) spray-painted a moral gloss of judgement over the descriptive wall of the facts. This was indeed David Hume's view:

"Vice and virtue may be compared to sounds, colours, heat and cold, which, according to modern philosophy, are not qualities in objects but perceptions in the mind ... moral judgments are a matter of the gilding and staining of]natural objects with the colours borrowed from internal sentiment." (Hume, Enquiry, appendix 1, 1983:88)

Exercise 10.4: you are invited to go with your friends to Kudos nightclub where you know there will be drunkenness and drug-taking. Your grandmother doesn't like the idea. You say, 'but Nan, it will be so much fun!".

Write your grandmother's reply (using the open question attack).

MacIntyre's Attack on Emotivism

In After Virtue (1974) Alasdair MacIntyre vigorously disputes the logical basis of emotivism and attempts to re-assert the truth and validity of naturalism. As a virtue ethicist broadly in the Aristotelean tradition (even though he rejects Aristotle's metaphysical biology and his doctrine of the Mean) MacIntyre sees ideas of goodness firmly rooted in the facts of **forms of life**, and the practices associated with different forms of life. If you like, this is a sociological origin of our ideas of goodness.

MacIntyre observes that:

"there seems to be no rational way of securing moral agreement in our culture." (2006:6).

Ill-sorted fragments of arguments jumble for prominence in people's minds. And one of these fragments is the pervasive influence of emotivism. Emotivism's legacy is to evacuate rational considerations from the argument. Agreement is to be found "by producing certain non-rational effects on the emotions" along the lines of Ayer's second function of emotive language - to sway someone to my own viewpoint.

MacIntyre levels the following criticisms at emotivism:

• Emotivists are strangely silent when asked to identify what emotions exactly are present when I say 'stealing is wrong". Is it anger? Or indifference? Or repulsion? Much the same could be said of approval, which takes many forms: rational assent is different for example to emotional empathy but both entail approval.

• Emotivists fail to distinguish between different types of statement, for example, differences between stating a preference and stating a judgement. So emotivism shrinks the breadth and diversity of language.

• Emotivists misunderstand the nature of meaning:

"The expression of feeling or attitude is characteristically a function not of the meaning of sentences, but of their use on particular occasions" (2006:13).

So, argues MacIntyre, whatever moral statements are doing they are not doing what Ayer describes them as doing.

Moral statements in ordinary usage are saying something very different from "hurray for honesty!" or "down with stealing!". In fact emotivism hides itself under the cloak of a theory of meaning when it is in fact an empirical thesis about how our human psychology works, culturally located at a time in philosophical development of the turn of the nineteenth century. It is a child of its times, and "we live in a specifically emotivist culture" (2006:22).

Macintyre's project is to establish that "genuine objective and impersonal moral standards can be rationally justified" (2006:19). The fact that our culture tends to take moral statements as statements of personal preference, of an extreme relativistic sort, does not mean that this is the only way to view moral discourse. The sweeping conclusion that all rational justifications for a universal morality have failed is a fallacious conclusion.

Exercise 10.5: Summarise MacIntyre's attack on emotivism.

Further Problems with Ayer's View

1. Eliminates a lot of **language-games** that we play – such as poetry, God-talk, as well as morality.

2. The **verification principle** cannot be verified, is neither analytic nor synthetic, and so is **meaningless** in its own terms.

3. **Prescriptivism**, a theory developed by RM Hare, argues for a Kantian view of language – that moral uses of good have within them the idea that the statement should be **universalised**. "Killing is wrong means – you shouldn't kill, that's my strong advice, and I shouldn't kill either". It is prescribing a consistent course of action which implies a shared understanding of universal precepts (such as 'do not kill').

4. **Analytic/synthetic** distinction has problems in reality. Hume talks about analytic statements being 'associations of ideas'. But it depends which ideas we 'associate' or link together. Example: before Australia was discovered 'all swans are white' appears to be analytic. But when black

swans were found it becomes synthetic. We can no longer associate 'colour, with 'swanhood' analytically (as a part of the definition).

John Searle's Naturalistic Argument from the Idea of Language-Games

Jon Search employs the following argument to demonstrate how we move from descriptive 'is' statements to prescriptive 'ought' statements.

- You lend Brian £1000

- Brian promises to pay back the loan on January 1st

- Brian doesn't pay the loan back by the due date

- Brian ought to pay the loan back because he's signed up to the language game of promising, which involves strict obligations to do what you say.

Therefore we have moved from a descriptive 'is' statement (Brian promises to pay the money back) to an ought statement (Brian **should** pay it back) - the link is "Brian has opted into the language game of promising which includes certain social obligations such as keeping your word, truth-telling, and developing trust.

Thought-point: You can link this to Wittgenstein's theory of language-games in Philosophy of Religion

Exercise 10.6: Naturalists have a defence against the naturalistic fallacy attack. What is this defence?

Naturalism and Absolutism

Do naturalists in ethics necessarily hold to absolute values?

It depends what we mean by 'absolute'. Absolute has three meanings - objective, non-consequentialist and universal.

Clearly situation ethics and utilitarians believe in an absolute norm (agape love and happiness respectively) but on the second meaning (non-consequentialist), they would be relativists as they believe that norms must be determined consequentially by evaluating the results of actions.

Kant is a **non-naturalist**, but believes in objective values, is non-consequentialist and also believes ethics is a universal, shared process of a priori reason determining the right action and obeying it by a 'good will'. So the non-naturalist Kant is actually absolute in all three meanings, whereas other naturalists are only absolute in two of the three.

Emotivism and Relativism

Are emotivists like AJ Ayer relativists? It depends what we mean by relativist. Relativism has three meanings.

Subjective - where values are up to me. Arguably emotivism is subjective as it argues that the ethical statement is an expression of a subjective response to something - approval or revulsion.

Particular to culture - emotivism has nothing much to say about the relation of feelings to culture as it is a theory of moral language and what good means, not a theory of ethical origins of where values come from.

Consequentialist - values are relative to consequences. In other words we cannot determine right and wrong without a situation and an outcome in view. There can be no absolute rules. Emotivism has nothing to say about this: it isn't a normative theory of ethics, but a theory of meaning of moral terms like 'good' and 'bad'.

Exercise 10.7: "Emotivists are relativists and naturalists absolutists". Explain how it isn't as simple as this.

Essay-writing Skill

Exercise 10.6: You need to practise unpacking the non-technical language as well as the technical vocabulary in the specification. In the question below (set in the old OCR specification in 2015, but still valid), the non-technical phrase is 'more useful than'. More useful than what, and for whom and for what purpose? Try an opening paragraph that unpacks both the technical language and the non-technical language below.

"Meta-ethics is **more useful than** normative ethics". Discuss

Conscience

"The person who launched the concept of conscience into the currency of our language was St Paul'. (Neville Symington, The Blind Man Sees, page 42)

Four Potential Sources of Conscience

- God – synderesis

- Reason – judgement

- Upbringing – Freud

- Evolution – Dawkins

Aquinas (Innate and Reasonable)

Two Words for Conscience (Aquinas)

- Synderesis

- Conscientia

Conscience is 'right reason in agreement with nature' (Aquinas).

It is both **innate** (we're born with synderesis) and a **process** of reason as the practice of wisdom sharpens up **conscientia**– working out secondary precepts to live by and then what to do when two 'goods' conflict.

"The orthodox view is that wherever two courses of action are possible, conscience tells me which is right, and to choose the other is sin". Bertrand Russell (1974:190)

Thomas Aquinas defines 'conscience' as the "application of knowledge to activity" (Summa Theologiae, I-II, I).

The knowledge comes through **synderesis**, which he regards as the natural disposition of the human mind by which we understand the basic principles of behaviour.

For Aquinas the conscience applies these primary precepts of synderesis to particular situations. The principles of synderesis are general. Examples are "Do good and avoid evil", 'Preserve life' and "Obey God."

To guide behaviour, conscience requires principles that are specific. These "secondary precepts" are derived from experience and instruction through developing practical wisdom (**phronesis**).

Phronesis is a life-skill we develop as we apply general primary precepts to particular circumstances and involves **the correct perception** of individual circumstances. (Source: Stanford Encyclopaedia)

Exercise 11.1: Explain the relationship between synderesis and conscientia

---

Application to Sexual Desire

"It is not the knowledge of the universal but only the evaluation of our feelings, which is not so excellent, that is dragged about by passion." (Aquinas, Commentary on the Nicomachean Ethics, Book 7, lecture 3, paragraph 1352)

- Universal, shared knowledge of goodness – **synderesis**

- Particular – using wisdom (phronesis/prudence) to work out what to do

- Here prudence fails us because of lust

- Weak-willed person – hasn't developed the skill of judging by **wisdom**

Vincible and Invincible Ignorance

- Vincible – we can be blamed for not finding out

- Invincible – we can't be blamed for not finding out (the knowledge was not available to us)

Exercise 11.2: In sexual ethics, how might invincible ignorance be applied?

Freud - Conscience in Conflict

"Conscience points out the difference between right and wrong and when violated inflicts a certain amount of suffering and disturbance". E Lecky (1913:62)

External authority is internalised through our upbringing aged 3-5 years. Fear of loss of love is internalised, and the child seeks to please the parent (or transfers parental authority to God).

Id – source of our instincts and passions, where **Eros**, the creative life force is in conflict with **Thanatos**, the source of death and destruction. Eros is driven by the gratification of the **pleasure principle**. The death instinct is 'the urge to restore an earlier state of things (Freud, Beyond the Pleasure Principle, page 308) ie non-being or annihilation of the self. Also linked in Freud to power, domination and aggression.

In the modern age we might also link Thanatos to self-harm, addiction and suicide.

Ego – formed by the **reality principle** as an individual expresses their own identity in pragmatic terms – in conformity with social expectations.

In the modern age we might link the ego to false conceptions of self created by advertising and to diseases such as anorexia.

Superego – has a 'judicial function which is called conscience' (Outline to Psychoanalysis page 205). The superego has three roles: self-observation, conscience and realisation of an ideal. Internalisation of **Thanatos**, the death instinct, requires a constraint – the superego. (Why War? Page 211). **Pleasure principle** also needs restraining. Superego restrains the infantile id and the immature ego.

The superego forms in early childhood aged 3-5 years as adults try to restrain the child's desire for self-gratification by praise and blame. Bad parenting can produce a distorted superego that feels guilty about things most people would see as irrational eg masturbation.

Conclusion: pathological, irrational guilt, is easily induced by the **superego** as a means of social control (using the power of religion). Also this **conflict** between superego and id can be a source of neurosis and mental illness.

Exercise 11.2: Explain how conscience to Freud is like an iceberg.

The Bad Conscience

Bad conscience = Nazi Adolf Eichmann at his trial in Israel in 1963 saying "I had to obey orders". 'Bad' here is infantile and underdeveloped, seeking excuses, avoiding responsibility. Hannah Arendt talks of the 'banality of evil' – Eichmann's answers were just banal, simplistic, unthinking, unreflective, basic (and inhuman). Arendt felt the lack of reflection (reason) and feelings (of sympathy) made the answer Eichmann gave 'banal'.

"Our conscience, far from being the implacable judge moralists are talking about, is by its origins, social anxiety and nothing more". Sigmund Freud

Exercise 11.3 Compare the theories of conscience of Freud and Aquinas. Complete the table comparing Aquinas and Freud for categories of origin, process and outcome.

	Freud	Aquinas
Origin	Upbringing age 3-5 years	God - innate synderesis
Process	Superego forms out of praise and blame and seeks to internalise eros and thanatos and judge between contrary forces	Conscientia - right reason in agreement with nature, or synderesis, confirms what to do in solving moral dilemmas
Outcome	Superego easily becomes a 'bad conscience' which simply reflects the will of an authority figure such as God, or Hitler in the case of Eichmann's trial	We can only follow apparent goods - recognition of actual evil is a logical impossibility as all actions are believed to be good
Evaluation for myself		
Evaluation for society		

Further reading: Walter A. Davis in *Deracination: Historicity, Hiroshima, and the Tragic Imperative* and *Death's Dream Kingdom: The American Psyche since 9/11.*

Essay-writing

Each section of the syllabus has a section of issues related (here to conscience). A study of conscience requires a comparison between Aquinas and Freud:

- on the concept of guilt

- on the presence or absence of God within the workings of the conscience and super-ego

- on the process of moral decision-making

    - whether conscience is linked to, or separate from, reason and the unconscious mind

    - whether conscience exists at all or is instead an umbrella term covering various factors involved in moral decision-making, such as culture, environment, genetic predisposition and education

These suggested issues can easily be turned into exam questions using the trigger words: discuss, compare, evaluate, critically compare, consider.

1. Critically evaluate the theories of conscience of Aquinas and Freud.

2. "Conscience is given by God, not formed by childhood experience". Critically evaluate this view with reference to Freud and Aquinas.

3. "Conscience is a product of culture, environment, genetic predisposition and education". Discuss

4. "Conscience is another word for irrational feelings of guilt". Discuss

5. "Freud's theory of conscience has no scientific basis. It is merely hypothesis". Discuss

6. 'Guilt feelings are induced by social relationships as a method of control". Discuss

7. Sample question 2017 "Conscience is just the superego". Discuss

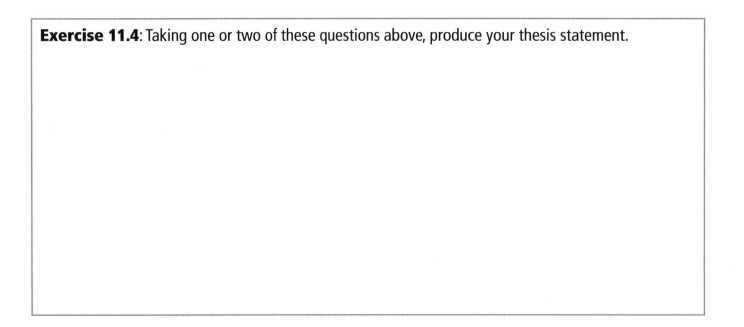

Exercise 11.4: Taking one or two of these questions above, produce your thesis statement.

Sexual Ethics

"The Church, nevertheless, in urging men to the observance of the precepts of the natural law, which it interprets by its constant doctrine, teaches that each and every marital act must of necessity retain its intrinsic relationship to the procreation of human life." Humanae Vitae, 1968, 12

Issues in Sexual Ethics

• **Autonomy** (set against social responsibility and in the light of Mill's harm principle – the only time we should restrict individual liberty is to prevent harm to others)

• **Social context of sexual relations** – family life, nature of individual liberty, child rearing responsibilities, disease prevention

• **Humanity** (what does it mean to be human? Do we have an unlimited right to our own expression of sexuality? Is there more than a procreative role for sexual relations eg communication/friendship). Does sex have a spiritual purpose (ie a higher purpose?).

• **Consent and respect** – Kant's second formula (of ends) suggest we should never treat anyone just as a means of getting pleasure but always as an 'end in themselves', as if we were that person ourself.

• **Pleasure -** sex is natural and pleasurable but does this mean we avoid responsibility for others?

Exercise 12.1 Examine the following diagram. How would you define 'true love' and do you agree it has three dimensions - intimacy, commitment and passion?

Varieties of Sexual Expression

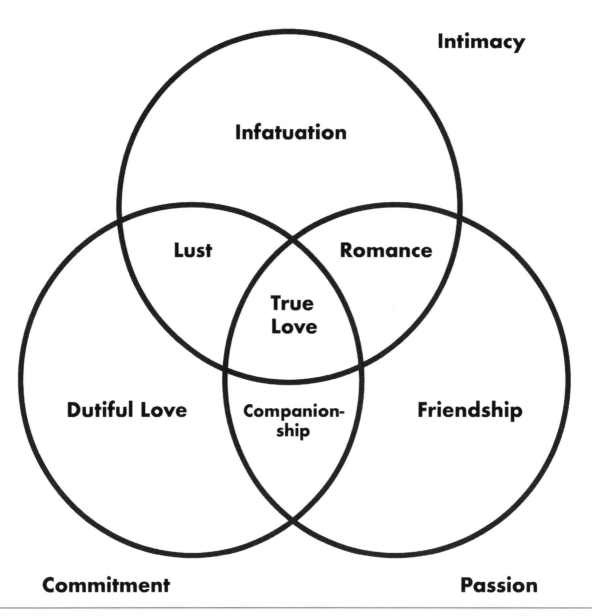

Intimacy

Infatuation

Lust   Romance

True
Love

Dutiful Love   Companion-
ship   Friendship

Commitment   **Passion**

Exercise 12.2: Are there any words missing from the above diagram? To what extent does the diagram illustrate that sex is both physical and spiritual?

Four Models of Sexual Ethics
1. Pleasure Model

Compare the situation today with two hundred years ago and try to understand how the utilitarian pleasure/pain scales have shifted.

1818 <————————————————————————————————————> 2018	
No effective contraception	
Sexual diseases widespread	
Women have little autonomy/power	
Religious prohibitions strong	
Homosexual relations illegal	
Social taboo against illegitimacy strong	

Exercise 12.3: Fill in the table above for social attitudes and laws in 2018

Exercise 12.4: How has the utilitarian balance shifted in 200 years (pleasure versus pain?)

2. Teleological Fulfilment and Spiritual Unity Model

Fulfilling sex transforms what could be a pleasurable and merely mechanical event into an expression of intimacy and love.

Sex is not just about a physical aspect (procreation). Does natural law theory fragment the concept of sex?

Catholic Church recognises the 'unitive and procreative' functions – but which comes first?

"The intimacy of love is the point to which desire naturally leads, by its own devices…it is a natural continuation of sexual pleasure to pursue such knowledge—to aim one's words, caresses and glances, as it were, into the heart of the other, and to know him or her from the inside, as a creature who is part of oneself." (Roger Scruton, Sexual Desire, page 92)

3. Communication Model

"Sexuality is primarily a means of communicating with other people, a way of talking to them, of expressing our feelings about ourselves and them. It is essentially a language, a body language, in which one can express gentleness and affection, anger and resentment, superiority and dependence far more succinctly than would be possible verbally'. (John Colbourne)

How people talk about sex is an important topic for public health researchers. After all, people who are uncomfortable asking their partners to wear a condom may be at higher risk of having unprotected sex and exposing themselves to sexually transmitted infections. Communication is also key to having enjoyable sexual encounters, Elizabeth Babin said.

But little research has delved into what keeps people from talking about their likes and dislikes while in bed, she said.

"In order to increase communication quality, we need to figure out why people are communicating and why they're not communicating," Babin said.

To do so, Babin recruited 207 people, 88 from undergraduate classes and 119 from online sites, to complete surveys about their apprehension about sexual communication, their sexual satisfaction and the amount of non-verbal and verbal communication they felt they enacted during sex. For example, participants were asked how much they agreed with statements such as, "I feel nervous when I think about talking with my partner about the sexual aspects of our relationship," and "I feel anxious when I think about telling my partner what I dislike during sex."

The participants, whose average age was 29, also responded to questions about their sexual self-esteem, such as how good a partner they felt they were and how confident they were in their sexual skills.

The surveys revealed that apprehension in talking about sex can spoil one's sexual enjoyment, with that anxiety linked both to less communication in bed and less satisfaction overall. Unsurprisingly, less sexual communication apprehension and higher sexual self-esteem were both associated with more communication during sex.

Communication during sex, in turn, was linked to more sexual satisfaction. Nonverbal communication was more closely linked to satisfaction than verbal communication, Babin reported online in August in the Journal of Social and Personal Relationships. Nonverbal cues may seem safer, Babin said.

"It could be perceived as being less threatening, so it might be easier to moan or to move in a certain way to communicate that I'm enjoying the sexual encounter than to say, 'Hey, this feels really good, I like that,'" Babin said. "That might seem too direct for some people." (source: Live Science)

4. Duty Model

Kant argues for duties that come from two elements - universalisability and the means/end formula.

Duties might include:

a. Treating the other person as if you were that person (are there dangers in this if you have perverted or unusual desires?)

b. Universalising your behaviour - but is it possible to have universalisable categorically such as 'never sleep with someone on your first date' or 'always use contraception'?

Is one of the difficulties with sexual relations that some of desires are **gender-specific** and it may be difficult therefore to abstract away from our desires (as Kant asks us to do) to a **universalisable** desire for different genders?

Exercise 12.5: Can we integrate these four ethical models into a holistic view of sex? For example, in having an implicit sexual statement of rights and duties?

Roman Catholic uses of Natural Law – a Design Argument (Teleological)

Humanae Vitae (1968) recognises two functions – the unitive and the procreative function of sex.

1. Humanae Vitae makes a bold claim: "In preserving intact the whole moral law of marriage, the Church is convinced that she is contributing to the creation of a truly human civilisation."

2. Humanae Vitae argues only in marriage are the **unitive** and **procreative** function combined. Pre-marital sex therefore betrays the designed purpose of sex – to be enjoyed in faithfulness and lifelong commitment to the end of having and raising children.

3. Disagreement on sexual ethics followed Vatican II (1962) and was suppressed. Eighty-seven Catholic academics opposed Humanae Vitae (1968) on issues such as pre-marital sex, arguing that the Catholic position should be to support pre-marital sex in committed relationships and gay marriage.

Humanae Vitae links sexual ethics to the **intrinsic good** of reproduction, so concluding that pre-marital sex and contraception are wrong as they break the primary precept. Homosexual behaviour is seen as 'intrinsically disordered'.

Evaluation of Humanae Vitae 1968

1. Humanae Vitae implies a **rank ordering** of precepts because living in an ordered society might include strengthening the bond between human beings, by having a more open attitude to pre-marital sexual relations (less judgementalism, more honesty, less guilt).

2. Physicalism – a stress primarily on the physical and **procreative** aspects of sex and not enough on the 'unitive' (bonding, friendship) or even 'spiritual' aspects of sex. Isn't sex more about expressions of love than a physical act?

3. Humanae Vitae talks about the '**inviolable law**' or unbreakable secondary precepts. Aquinas never intends secondary precepts (no sex before marriage) to be unbreakable. They are applications of human reason and so subject to re-evaluation.

Issues in Human Sexuality (Church of England 2003)

Fundamental teaching and principles:

1. "Homosexual orientation in itself is no bar to a faithful Christian life or to full participation in lay and ordained ministry in the Church" (2007 General Synod motion)

2. "That sexual intercourse is an act of total commitment which belongs properly within a permanent married relationship; that fornication and adultery are sins against this ideal, and are to be met by a call to repentance and the exercise of compassion; that homosexual genital acts also fall short of this ideal, and are likewise to be met by a call to repentance and the exercise of compassion" (1987 General Synod motion).

3. In relation to marriage: "The Church of England's long standing teaching and rule are set out in Canon B30: 'The Church of England affirms, according to our Lord's teaching, that marriage is in its nature a union permanent and lifelong, for better for worse, till death them do part, of one man with one woman, to the exclusion of all others on either side, for the procreation and nurture of children, for the hallowing and right direction of the natural instincts and affections, and for the mutual society, help and comfort which the one ought to have of the other, both in prosperity and adversity'." (2014 on marriage, para 1)

Think About

"Religious positions are intended to preserve the sanctity of sex, they can actually create the opposite effect, losing balance between body and spirit, blurring the importance of healthy emotions and relationships—all equally important to sexual health." Psychology Today

---

Exercise 12.6: How does the Church of England teaching differ from the Roman Catholic view?

The Bible Seems to Mention Four Aspects of Sex

- **Procreation** "And God blessed them; and God said to them, 'Be fruitful and multiply " (**Genesis 1:28**)

- **Friendship** "On my bed night after night I sought him whom my soul loves". (**Song of Songs 3:1**)

- **Passion** "May he kiss me with the kisses of his mouth! For your love is better than wine." (**Song of Songs 1:2**)

- **Fulfilment** "And they became one flesh". (**Genesis 2:24**)

Research: Father Harden defends Humanae Vitae in this account http://www.therealpresence.org/archives/Faith_and_Morals/Faith_and_Morals_003.htm

A Catholic sexual abuse victim responds to Humanae Vitae

http://www.catholicsandcontraception.com/humanae-vitae-in-catholic-clairs-life/

Stephen Fry attacks the Catholic position on homosexuality

https://www.youtube.com/watch?v=zIgnw-b2Oro

A Sexual Bill of Rights

Humanists would point to the possibility of drawing up a **Sexual Health Bill of Rights and Responsibilities**.

Sexual Rights

- I have the right to own my own body.

- I have a right to my own feelings, beliefs, opinions and perceptions.

- I have a right to trust my own values about sexual conduct.

- I have a right to set my own sexual limits

- I have a right to say no.

- I have a right to say yes.

- I have a right to experience sexual pleasure.

- I have a right to remain celibate.

- I have a right to be sexually assertive.

- I have a right to be the initiator in a sexual relationship.

- I have a right to be in control of my sexual experiences.

- I have a right to have a loving partner.

- I have a right to my sexual orientation and preferences.

- I have a right to have a partner who respects me, understands me, and is willing to communicate with me.

- I have a right to talk to my partner about incest/child sexual abuse/rape.

- I have a right to ask questions and receive accurate sexual information.

Sexual Responsibilities

Each person has the responsibility to:

- respect the rights of other people

- honour the decisions and choices of others

- respect his/her sexual partner

- consider the feelings of his/her sexual partner

- make personal choices and decisions rather than being talked into actions which cause guilty or uneasy feelings

- take and share the actions necessary for sexual health

- share the decisions and actions regarding birth control

- never pressure anyone into any sexual activity

- never use sexual experiences as a threat, manipulation or punishment

- never have sex with children

Exercise 12.7: Using the previous list evaluate how the major ethical theories you have studied might integrate (or perhaps not integrate) this list of rights and responsibilities.

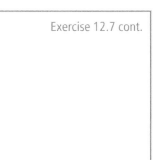

Essay-writing Practice

"Kantian ethics is the best approach to issues surrounding sexual behaviour". Discuss

Write a timed essay in 35 minutes on this title, carefully planning your essay before you start.

For a written example of an A grade answer, go to <u>Peped.org</u> Philosophy > Christian Thought > Kant

Activity - Research a Debate

Two academics, Roger Scruton and Martha Nussbaum on the role and place of sexual desire.

Roger Scruton has written a book on sexual desire, Sexual Desire: A Moral Philosophy of the Erotic (1986). He argues, that desire is a part of our characteristically human "intentionality"—that is, it is connected with the way we take a perspective on the world and react to things as we interpret them.

According to Scruton, the true or natural aim of sexual desire is only fully satisfied in deep erotic love. And since love is closely linked to **esteem**, and cannot coexist with the belief that its object is profoundly unworthy, the aim of love is itself, in turn, satisfied only in a stable relationship that is based on moral approval.

Scruton insists that this stable love can itself be best achieved and maintained **within the institution of marriage**, and that this institution can best be protected in a conservative society with a state religion.

Martha Nussbaum debates the central thesis of this book and comments:

Roger Scruton confuses two distinct claims: (1) the claim that sexual desire that does not aim at lasting spiritual union is second-rate; and (2) the claim that sexual desire that does not succeed in achieving a lasting spiritual relationship is second-rate.

Scruton repeatedly asserts that the deep spiritual intimacy of love is the "natural end" or "fulfilment" of sexual desire. (For example, page 92: "The intimacy of love is the point to which desire naturally leads, by its own devices…it is a natural continuation of sexual pleasure to pursue such knowledge—to aim one's words, caresses and glances, as it were, into the heart of the other, and to know him from the inside, as a creature who is part of oneself."

This already implies that there is something problematic about the person who deliberately chooses not to aim at love in his or her sexual life: for such a person will be turning away from the natural end of his or her own desire. But later on Scruton makes it very clear that his notion of the natural is a normative and moral notion, which gives rise to moral judgments about the worth of sexual activities.

He identifies his notion of "fulfilment" with Aristotle's concept of a natural telos ("end" or "goal"), and writes as follows:

Love is the fulfilment of desire, and therefore love is its telos. A life of celibacy may also be fulfilled; but, assuming the general truth that most of us have a powerful, and perhaps overwhelming, urge to make love, it is in our interests to ensure that love—and not some other thing—is made…. The fulfilment of sexual desire defines the nature of desire. And the nature of desire gives us our standard of normality. (Sexual Desire, page 339)

He argues, further, on the same page (339) that, since love can flourish only in a moral and social climate that supports fidelity, "a whole section of traditional sexual morality must be upheld."

In other words, according to Scruton's Aristotelian argument, love is to sexual desire as the mature flourishing life of a tree is to the young developing plant: the natural, healthy, normal end state for that process of development, which gives that process its point and defines its nature.

Now a human activity may fail to reach its telos in two different ways, as this passage points out.

It can be blocked from outside, as when the social institutions surrounding a person do not support his or her quest for fulfilment. In this case, as Scruton here argues, we have, according to his view, a moral reason to revise those institutions in order to make them supportive of our quest for our telos.

But an individual human being can also deliberately choose to aim his or her desire away from the natural telos, pursuing sexual pleasure without love.

In this case, it is Scruton's contention that the person is acting against his or her deep human interests, and (if this is not an isolated occurrence—cf. page 290) is morally blameworthy.

Since Scruton does not hold that all such people are so blameworthy as to be sexually perverted, "superficial and second-rate" seems to me an accurate, if mild, summary of his general condemnation. (Scruton's point about celibacy—cf. also pages 320–321—is mysterious, since on an Aristotelian view deliberate non-use should be just as bad as divergent use.)

It is a central aim of Scruton's book to establish that a correct understanding of the nature of sexual desire yields moral judgments, in which the pursuit of love is ranked, as a sexual enterprise, above promiscuous and otherwise loveless pleasure seeking (pages 290, 338).

His claim about the telos of desire is crucial to that argument.

source http://www.nybooks.com/articles/1987/05/07/sexual-desire-an-exchange/Postscript

Revisiting the DARM Approach

The **DARM** approach to ethics outlined i chapter 1 is a simple way of encouraging analysis and evaluation. We need to understand clearly how norms (values of goodness) are derived (**D** for Derivation) by different theories, and how the norm so derived is then applied to an ethical issue (**A** for Application).

We can evaluate as we go along: is the process of derivation by this theory logical and clear? If I try living by this theory for one day, how does it feel?

There are some base questions which we need to answer in ethics:

1.   What do I do when two moral 'goods' conflict? If I am tempted to lie to save the reputation of a friend, loyalty to my friend is in conflict with telling the truth.

Exercise 13.1: Fill in the table.

	What happens when two moral 'goods' conflict?
Kantian Ethics	
Natural Law	
Situation Ethics	
Utilitarianism	

2. What problems, if any, are there in applying the norms produced by these theories?

Exercise 13.2: Fill in the Table below.

	Problems of applying the ethical norm
Kantian Ethics	
Natural Law	
Situation Ethics	
Utilitarianism	

The **R** of **DARM** stands for realism. How realistic is this theory in terms of our understanding of human nature and psychology? What would Freud say about each of our theories?

3. Is it true to our psychology that, as Kant argues, feelings are irrelevant to moral decision-making? Was Hume right in arguing 'reason is the slave of the passions'?

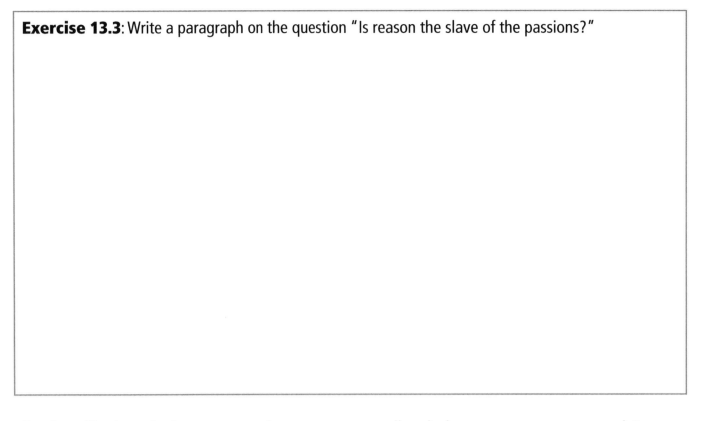

Exercise 13.3: Write a paragraph on the question "Is reason the slave of the passions?"

For the utilitarians, the issues seem to be two - can we really calculate consequences accurately? Utilitarianism seems to work fine looking backwards, for example, in 1967 assessing the effects of illegal backstreet abortions in terms of human misery and death. But what about looking forwards?

And secondly, does utilitarianism always put individual rights behind the general happiness? Can utilitarians like Mill successfully get around the criticism posed by Bernard Williams in his example of Jim and the Indians?

In Natural Law theory we need to be careful not to confuse the Roman Catholic interpretation of Natural law with what Aquinas actually argues. For example, Aquinas does not argue that secondary precepts (applications by reason of the general primary precepts) are absolute and inviolable. Yet Roman Catholicism argues that abortion and euthanasia are inviolably evil. They are absolute wrongs.

This difference between Aquinas and modern Catholicism is not accidental. It arises because, from the 1960s, the Catholic church has seen relativism as the arch-enemy of universal, absolute norms given by God.

So just before he was elected Pope, Benedict spoke of the 'tyranny of relativism'. He implied by this that there was a lack of tolerance for anyone who argues for absolute unchangeable truth and unbreakable norms. Free speech on such issues had been closed down, he felt.

But is the Catholic Church being realistic in arguing for no contraception when many of its own followers clearly practise contraception? In an overpopulated world, is this stance against contraception actually justifiable as 'moral'?

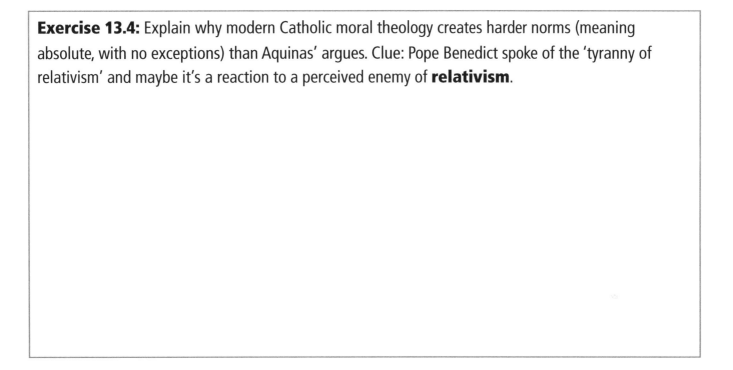

Exercise 13.4: Explain why modern Catholic moral theology creates harder norms (meaning absolute, with no exceptions) than Aquinas' argues. Clue: Pope Benedict spoke of the 'tyranny of relativism' and maybe it's a reaction to a perceived enemy of **relativism**.

The **M** of **DARM** stands for Motivation. Why should I be moral and not simply a selfish egoist?

The Utilitarians follow David Hume in arguing that I am moral put of a feeling of sympathy for fellow-human beings. I don't like to see them suffer,, so I sacrifice altruistically on their behalf.

Joseph Fletcher argues I commit by faith to the cause of love because I believe it to be the best norm.

Kant argues I am moral out of a sense of awe for the moral law within me - part of my rational capacity as a human being.

Natural law theory hold I am moral because God has imparted within me the intuitive knowledge of right and wrong and by my very nature as human I orientate myself towards good ends - the teleological basis of natural law. Aquinas calls this **synderesis**.

Notice however that this view is disputed within the Christian tradition. Evangelical Christians argue the imago dei is so obscured and distorted by sin that I cannot find God by myself unless God finds me first. Both views come from St Paul. For example, Paul seems to argue for synderesis in Romans 2:14,

Indeed, when Gentiles, who do not have the Law, do by nature what the Law requires, they are a law to themselves, even though they do not have the Law, since they show that the work of the Law is written on their hearts, their consciences also bearing witness, and their thoughts either accusing or defending them. (Romans 2:14, NIV)

But Paul also argues in Romans 7 that we are all sold under sin to a slavery to evil, and that nothing good dwells within me. My 'flesh' is fatally corrupted by sin. This seems to suggest an imago dei which is almost blotted out entirely. Calvin struggles with this issue (see Christian Thought paper H573/3 section on Knowledge of God and Calvin's view on **sensus divinitatis**).

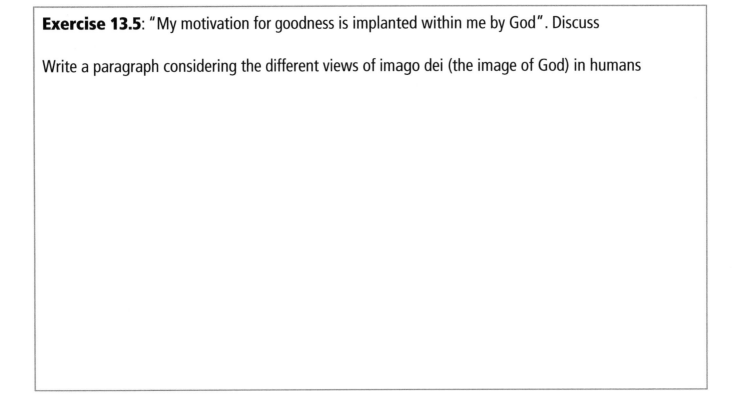

Exercise 13.5: "My motivation for goodness is implanted within me by God". Discuss

Write a paragraph considering the different views of imago dei (the image of God) in humans

About the Author

Peter Baron is well-known in the UK as a trainer, educator and writer on Philosophy and Ethics as well as a first-rate teacher.

He read Politics, Philosophy and Economics at New College, Oxford and afterwards obtained an MLitt for a research degree in Hermeneutics at Newcastle University. He qualified as an Economics teacher in 1982, and taught ethics at Wells Cathedral School in Somerset from 2006-2012. From 2012 he ahs been a freelance writer and speaker.

In 2007 he set up a philosophy and ethics community dedicated to enlarging the teaching of philosophy in schools by applying the theory of multiple intelligences to the analysis of philosophical and ethical problems. So far over 700 schools have joined the community and over 40,000 individuals use his website every month.

To join the community please register your interest by filling in your details on the form on the website. We welcome contributions and suggestions so that our community continues to flourish and expand.

www.peped.org contains **EXTRACTS** and **FURTHER READING** mentioned in the exam specification, plus additional articles, handouts and essay plans. Notice that the exam specification merely gives guidance as to further reading - you may use any source or philosopher you find relevant to the construction of your argument. Indeed, if you have the courage to abandon the selection (and any examples) introduced by your textbook, you will relieve the examiner of boredom and arguably launch yourself on an A grade trajectory.

Links, reviews, news and revision materials available on www.peped.org

www.peped.org website allows students and teachers to explore Philosophy of Religion and Ethics through handouts, film clips, presentations, case studies, extracts, games and academic articles.

Pitched just right, and so much more than a text book, here is a place to engage with critical reflection whatever your level. Marked student essays are also posted.

Published by Active Education

www.peped.org

First published in 2018

ISBN: 9781983148989

Cartoons used with permission © Becky Dyer

All images © their respective owners

Printed in Great Britain
by Amazon

The Ethics Study Guide is designed to help GCE A level students ask the right questions by unpacking key theories and applications according to structures of thought, and by doing the exercises, to build essay-writing skills step by step.

By analysing assumptions and worldviews, and making principles crystal clear, the student is able to build an ethics toolkit which can help answer questions on any applied issue.

Business ethics, euthanasia and sexual ethics are considered as appleid issues, including discussions on how the major ethical theories of Kant, the utilitarians Bentham and Mill, Fletcher's situation ethics, and Aquinas' natural law theory.

Detailed evaluation helps build the critical sense and the book comes with its own website of additional material, peped.org.

An essential book for those who wish to be liberated to think philosophically, with rigour and flexibility.

Visit http://peped.org for more resources.

ISBN 9781983148989

9 781983 148989

Peped